PLANNING FOR SUCCESS

LIVE

YOUR

DREAM

D1316740

PLANNING FOR SUCCESS

LIVE *YOUR* DREAM

DR. MARK J. CHIRONNA

DESTINY IMAGE® PUBLISHERS, INC.
P.O. Box 310, Shippensburg, PA 17257-0310
"Speaking to the Purposes of God for This Generation and for the Generations to Come."

This book and all other Destiny Image, Revival Press, MercyPlace, Fresh Bread, Destiny Image Fiction, and Treasure House books are available at Christian bookstores and distributors worldwide.

For a U.S. bookstore nearest you, call 1-800-722-6774.
For more information on foreign distributors, call 717-532-3040.
Reach us on the Internet: www.destinyimage.com.

ISBN 10: 0-7684-3102-6
ISBN 13: 978-0-7684-3102-5

For Worldwide Distribution, Printed in the U.S.A.
1 2 3 4 5 6 7 8 9 10 11 / 13 12 11 10 09

DEDICATION

To my sons, Matthew and Daniel,
My highest aspiration, my ultimate prayer, is for you to live your dreams.

ACKNOWLEDGMENTS

Thank you to:

My wife, Ruth, for your unending inspiration and encouragement.

Destiny Image for believing in this book and in me.

Misty Durnell for your stellar administrative support.

Donna Scuderi for your seamless work.

Carol Bailey for your diligent transcribing.

The Master's Touch family. I have been privileged to walk through these truths with you. Thank you for your tenacity, faithfulness, and love.

ENDORSEMENT

The psalmist teaches us to delight ourselves in the Lord and He will give us the desires of our heart. This is a truth for believers in every generation. Master teacher, senior pastor, and life coach Mark Chironna takes this principle and gives us practical tools to help unlock our destinies. This enlightening book will help you envision your strategic life, enable you to write your life's plan, and cultivate faith within you so you will watch your destiny unfold before your very eyes. Do not settle for a boring, mundane Christian life! Arise to the occasion, and be all you can be in Christ Jesus!

James W. Goll
Founder, Encounters Network
and Prayer Storm International
Author, *The Seer, The Lost Art of Intercession,
The Coming Israel Awakening,* and others

Live Your Dream is a must-read for every person who wants to move forward in their lives. His advice and counsel will inspire you to dream and provoke you to take action. I consider Dr. Mark Chironna to be one the clarion "voices" of the 21st century. I advise everyone to answer the call that God is making through this important and prophetic revelation.

Pastor Suzette Caldwell, Associate Pastor
Author, *Praying to Change Your Life*

Live Your Dream is not just another self-help book; it's not just another *how to be better in business* tome. Yes, it's full of useful advice, historic examples, and vitally important knowledge about how to recognize and achieve your life's dreams, but what I love most about the book is that it courageously proclaims that living out your destiny is not merely a luxury for the few, it's not just a God-given right; in fact, it is a responsibility for all of us—a responsibility to ourselves, to others we are in relationship with, and to the rest of humanity, both alive and yet unborn. It's like a really good cup of coffee—it'll get you going.

Simon T. Bailey
Author, *Release Your Brilliance*

Live Your Dream is an uplifting work that leads readers to rediscover their dreams. In fact, Dr. Chironna uses this work to show people that it's not only OK to dream, it's vital if they want to walk in their destinies. This book helps readers understand that the good *and* bad times contribute to the big picture—a life of purpose. Through fascinating anecdotes and relatable examples, Dr. Chironna shows how aspirations, activity, and attitude lead to actualization. This is a great motivational tool that says more than, "Go team!" It teaches readers to have faith in something larger than themselves, and it proves how faith can move mountains.

Bishop Eddie Long

Possibly one of the greatest needs of the Church today is for vision to complete the objective, the goal. In order to accomplish what God has planned for our lives, we must do just as this book tells us: embrace our dreams and open up the gateway for the fulfillment of our destinies by employing the gifts God has placed within us. Dr. Mark Chironna has presented a powerful message; every person in the world can take something from these pages and become the success God intended!

Dr. Stephan K. Munsey, Senior Pastor
Family Christian Center
Munster, Indiana

Dr. Mark has the master's touch of fusing spiritual revelation with practical relevance. He offers powerful insights yet with practical applications—inspiration followed with precise instruction. The missing link to most books on successful living is strategy! Like a dream engineer, Dr. Mark will have you writing, watching, and walking out the dreams of your life—strategically. Rarely will you find a writer with both skilled intelligence and sensitive intuitiveness. Dr. Mark Chironna is truly a gentleman and a scholar. This book may be the last book you will need to start your life's mission.

Phil Munsey

TABLE OF CONTENTS

PART I

ENVISION YOUR STRATEGIC LIFE

UNCORK YOUR DREAM

There is nothing like a dream to create the future.[1] —Victor Hugo

You are one of a kind. Of the billions of people born since time began, *no one* compares to you. Your family name may be commonplace. You may have your granddad's eyes. You might even be an identical twin; yet you are a unique creation whose features, characteristics, abilities, and sensibilities are factored together in such a way as to make you a creation without match.

That is precisely why you are reading this page. There is encoded within you something powerful, something no one else has, and it is stirring within your heart. You are simmering with potential and it is poised to collide with opportunity. The energy released by that auspicious impact will create exciting new paradigms and propel you toward your destiny.

Somewhere inside, you can already feel it. You may be highly accomplished and living the life you always wanted, yet sensing the power of untapped dreams still locked inside your heart. You may be a student, uncertain where life is headed, but brimming with confidence that your future is bright. Perhaps your life's picture is not as rosy as it once was. Bewildered, you find yourself in a parched field of broken dreams, overwhelmed by obstacles and difficulties, beaten down by disappointment and loss.

Whatever your circumstances and past experiences, there is infinite promise still ahead. Your dreams may be covered in dust, they may even be shattered into tiny pieces, but deep down you know the game clock is still running. Something inside you is saying, *As long as there is breath in my lungs, my dreams can come true.*

Listen to Your Dream

Sometimes the dream nestled in your heart sings with conviction, assurance, and vigor; but often it whispers. Either way, your dream is priceless and laden with significance. It is fundamentally linked to your destiny and its potential can hardly be imagined or described.

Once you set your dream in motion, it is capable of producing astounding results. A dream fulfilled changes the atmosphere of life. It contains the power to create, to revitalize, to cure a disease, to transform a life, to revolutionize technology, to foster hope and benefit the poor—your dream can change your world.

If your experiences have proven otherwise until now, you may find this statement hard to believe. Time and trouble may have taken their toll; your hope for the future may be worn thin. You may see your dreams as unimportant, inconsequential, or lost forever. Without realizing it, you may have buried your dreams under layers of self-rejection so deep you are no longer consciously aware of them.

But that is not the end of your story! The game clock *is* still running. Your dreams—even those that have been crushed or forgotten—can be activated at any time. Like seeds lying dormant for years, your dreams remain potent and full of life, packed with the intangible substance of your destiny!

If we will listen, our dreams will help us understand who we were created to be and what we were born to do. Consider your life's dream a "snapshot of the future" that awaits your arrival. Your dream can keep you motivated in bleak times and shed light on the path ahead, even when the path seems overrun with the rubble of the past.

With your dream firmly in mind and guiding your choices, your efforts will be honed to produce desirable, beneficial outcomes. Using your snapshot as your standard, you can evaluate your progress every step of the way and make adjustments designed to correct your course and manage shifting tides. *Your dream is a powerful image of your desired outcomes; it enables you to see the finish line from the starting gate.*

Everything that stands between you and your dream is subject to change. Adverse circumstances—obstacles, discouragement, even missteps—do not negate your future. Allow the snapshot your dream provides to revive your hope when days are difficult and the cares of life hijack your attention. Redirect your thoughts to the finish line. Focus on your potential to overcome adversity and you *will* arrive at your desired destination.

When your dreams are allowed to touch your imagination, they will inspire—and reinspire—your vision. Children do this instinctively; they have not yet learned to doubt or dismiss the dreams brewing in their youthful imagination. Daily their hopes soar, and so can yours.

Learn or relearn to treasure the desires of your heart because they are part of *you,* a person of limitless potential who is destined for fruitfulness. Allow your dreams to lead you, not to a stopping-off place where you will "make do" until your proverbial ship comes in, but to *the* place you really want to go...a place where you can flourish as a mighty oak tree planted beside a cool stream. Seek *your* place in this world, a bounteous place of fulfillment, peace, increase, liberality, and influence.

My desire as a life coach is for you to become an unabashed proponent of your destiny—a man, woman, or youth convinced of the truth that you are fearfully and wonderfully made and designed with boundless potential. I choose my words with care, not to stroke your ego or pump you up, but because they speak truthfully about your identity as a human being.

The very fact of your birth is irrefutable evidence of your significance. Your inherent value as a person exceeds that of any other creature or created thing. Untold worth resides within you; therefore, the outcomes of your life are consequential and planning for those outcomes is vital.

Listen to the dream embedded in your heart. It speaks to the person you are—a gifted, talented, creative individual infused with destiny and equipped with natural and supernatural means to fulfill it. Your dream speaks to "someone else" too: it is calling out to the person you are about to become, a person with a fully-engaged dream who is experiencing life— *radically.*

Live *Your* Dream

Your dream is also one of a kind, custom-tailored to your life's purpose. Your desires were not fitted to anyone but you. The things you long for will not satisfy your next-door neighbor. Likewise, the dreams which others pursue won't slake your thirst for significance and fulfillment.

In a world where celebrity, power, and wealth are touted as ends unto themselves, we can be drawn off course and enticed to model ourselves after people whom we consider to be successful. When we buy into media-generated ideas about how we should look, what we should desire, and how we ought to succeed, we find ourselves living someone else's life and coveting what someone else (whose destiny is distinct from our own) has.

Over the long haul, this pursuit of a counterfeit dream distracts us from our authentic purpose—the very thing that gives life to our desires. We can become so focused on impossible standards and misdirected goals that we lose sight of who we are. Media images barraging our minds can then convince us that we are something "less than" we should be. We can be tricked into playing out of position by modeling ourselves after unsuitable or even unreal examples.

Every professional athlete knows the value of playing in position. The principle can be most easily seen in team sports where each player is assigned a specific role based on individual strengths, abilities, affinity for the task, and overall team objectives. With each player covering their assigned turf, the team functions as a healthy, successful unit, and everyone involved is empowered to excel.

The baseball manager knows that putting the pitcher behind the plate instead of on the mound will disadvantage his team and cause discouragement, especially for the misplaced pitcher. Laden with catchers' gear and lacking the training needed to function in a new position, the pitcher will play nine exhausting innings outside his area of expertise. Meanwhile, his talent for throwing strikes will have been wasted and his team will suffer the consequences.

The professional pitcher has no desire to be a catcher. It's not the role for which he was built. Having a clear sense of professional identities is vital in any team sport. Each player must know *why* he or she is there. Ask an NHL goaltender whether he longs to score a goal. He will tell you that he lives not to rack up points, but to stand guard between the pipes and prevent others from scoring against his team.

Professional athletes, managers, and coaches know that by respecting each player's unique skill set and identity, the team will function at the highest level. The team can then play with clarity as to the desired end result and each athlete can contribute to the achievement of the team's shared goals.

When we apply these qualities and attitudes to our lives, we begin to live *strategically* so that we can realize our dreams and benefit from the journey.

Plan to Live Strategically

To live strategically simply means to have a picture of your desired outcomes in mind and to put a strategy in place to help you achieve them. It is a lifestyle that is anything but random. Strategic people don't hum the tune, "Que Sera Sera" (Whatever Will Be, Will Be). Instead they choose to live proactively and engage life fully, whatever the challenges. They don't see themselves as victims of chance. Instead, those who live strategically see themselves as being empowered to make choices that help shape their life outcomes. Strategic planners live *intentionally.*

Living intentionally is a lifestyle that harmonizes with your destiny. Your life is *not* an accident, *regardless of the circumstances surrounding your conception.* When you recognize and embrace this fundamental truth, you are empowered to become a more active participant in the formation of your future. Instead of wondering how your life will turn out, you become the architect of your destiny; you draw the plans and you live the dream.

Intentional living is also compatible with the desire to experience life to the full. We are most content, most productive, and most fulfilled when we pursue life with intentionality. When we step onto our intended paths, circumstances begin to fall into place and we enter the sublime and supernatural experience of being the right person in the right place at the right time—for the right reasons.

Strategic living is an individual pursuit. Your older brother may be an A-list attorney. You may be as bright as he is and you may come from a long line of lawyers, yet it doesn't necessarily follow that your purpose will be fulfilled in the practice of law. To live strategically means to choose the specific path that is right *for you* and then do the things that keep you moving along that path.

No one values strategy more than a war-time general. The wise commander can tell you that, although battle plans are always subject to change, having a plan in place remains the seasoned strategist's first priority. The stakes of war are high and outcomes are irreversible. Generals must have a clear picture of the overall goal and then develop a clear blueprint of the strategic and tactical steps that will help them achieve the desired victory.

Military leaders also understand that when a solid strategic plan is in place, the tactical steps required to implement overall objectives become practically self-evident. With clear strategic objectives to follow, it is much easier to make decisions about equipment, personnel, timelines, and troop movements. Commanding officers are therefore empowered to facilitate victory while minimizing casualties and preventing collateral damage.

The careful management of these details enables troops to fight another day in the hopes of achieving desired results. Plans at the tactical level, however, can fully succeed only when they are established within the context of a sound strategic plan.

The same is true in our personal lives. Managing life's day-to-day details helps us to keep our lives on track. We wash the dishes, balance our checkbooks, maintain our automobiles, and show up at work on time. These efforts keep us from slipping into chaos and becoming overwhelmed by the minutiae that is part of everyday life.

Yet as important as it is to stay on top of things, a smooth operation is not an end in itself. In fact, the real value of order is this: It creates a healthy routine and a sense of balance that frees you to pursue life's bigger picture. The metaphor of the forest and the trees applies: If you fail to maintain a macro view of your forest, the trees will prevent you from appreciating its larger design.

That is why having a strategic life plan is so critical. It helps you focus and find practical ways to achieve something amazing, something that seems beyond you and beyond the perceived limits of your abilities. A strategic plan opens hidden pathways you didn't even know existed. These new corridors will guide you around, over, and through your current circumstances and take you where you are destined to go.

Taste, Feel, Touch Your Dream

Your life is already rigged with the makings of a remarkable adventure. Not only did you come packaged with seeds of destiny, you also came equipped with superb mental and emotional faculties that can water those seeds and ignite your belief in something that, for the time being, exists only in your thoughts.

Faith in your dream, when combined with curiosity and imagination, can bring elements of the future into your present reality. First, realize that thinking about your destiny is not a waste of your time. Allow ideas about your future to enter your conscious thoughts. Think through your dream and verbalize it. Envision yourself there. Indulge your dream by paying attention to its details.

Do you desire to be a vice president of marketing for a major firm, perhaps your current firm? Then treat yourself to a full sensory experience by imagining the fine points of being in that position. What does it feel like to arrive in your corner office each day? What does it look like when the sun streams through your floor-to-ceiling windows and shines on the photos and awards that line your credenza? What does it smell like when you arrive in the morning to fresh-brewed coffee prepared by your faithful assistant?

Envision your destiny *and* consider on a practical level what it will take to get there. Learn from the example of others; assess the gifts, abilities, and talents of someone who is already successful in the position you desire. Begin to think like a marketing vice president thinks.

Then go a step further and behave your way into your future. Groom yourself day by day; prepare yourself to accept greater responsibility and work to increase your level of expertise. Take note of the current vice president's experiences and picture yourself wearing her shoes. Don't pray for her to retire early or lose her job; your dream is not dependent upon someone else's demise.

Instead, imagine yourself sitting at a desk like hers and making the kinds of decisions she makes. Meanwhile, be determined to be the best contributor you can possibly be, wherever you are. Give your best effort at every opportunity, and the day will come when your dream will be fulfilled in all the best ways.

Unleash Your Destiny

Your dream is yours and only yours to live. Metaphorically speaking, your dream is the umbilical cord that ties you to your fully-formed destiny. Realize that you are "expecting." Nurture the dream that is forming within you and live in constant anticipation of the day your dream bursts into the open.

Be determined to experience the breathtaking collision of potential and opportunity. Walk with purpose straight toward the impact zone and be ready to harness the creative energy your dream releases. Be open to the paradigm shifts that occur, and savor the experience as the world around you and the private world that exists within your heart come alive as never before.

Go ahead, uncork your dream and unleash your destiny! You and you alone were built to live your dream and taste of its fruits. You were born at precisely the right moment for the most exquisite of reasons. You have something to give that the rest of us need and you will be rewarded in ways you cannot yet imagine.

To paraphrase Victor Hugo, *there is nothing like your dream to create your future.*

DECODE YOUR DESTINY

*I have things in my head that are not like what anyone has taught
me—shapes and ideas so near to me—so natural to my way of
being and thinking. . . .* [1]—Georgia O'Keeffe

In Ranchos de Taos, New Mexico, stands a small but celebrated building, the San Francisco de Asis Church. The fortress-like adobe mission was built by Franciscan fathers over a period of more than four decades beginning in the 18th century and remains one of the most frequently depicted structures in the United States.

Countless artists have captured their impressions of the mission on canvas, but none as unforgettably as the American artist, Georgia O'Keeffe. Her paintings of the edifice express her unique interpretive gifts and are deemed the quintessential renderings of the mission.

Georgia O'Keeffe was one of a kind. She was clearly attuned to her gifts and her unique "way of being and thinking;" therefore, she perceived her subjects, recorded light and form, and applied pigment to canvas in a distinctive way. She realized that her approach to art was different, not by accident, but by design.

This legendary painter recognized her individuality as an asset and purposefully tapped into the DNA of her dreams. She assessed her individuality and reckoned with her artistic quirks. She owned her rare qualities and actively engaged them. She supported their development and dared to be original. At some point she decided that she was comfortable in her own artistic "skin." She allowed her life to yield its meaning and she forged ahead to become an exceptional artist. *She cracked her destiny code.*

When Georgia O'Keeffe stood before the San Francisco de Asis Church, she was unencumbered by the need to conform to someone else's artistic formula. Instead, she was at liberty to absorb the scene and filter its elements through *her* perceptions and sensibilities. She empowered herself to capture the church on canvas as only she could. She allowed her destiny code to work for her. She extracted its vitality, exploited its strengths, and left a legacy which has enriched our culture and brought pleasure to art lovers everywhere.

Your destiny code is also one of a kind. It is the system of symbols, signals, and patterns that you experience in your life, both in your thoughts and throughout your external circumstances. Included in your destiny code are your relationships and the providential connections that pave the way to your dreams. Your destiny code is woven into the fabric of your life and is reflected in the unique events which you have experienced. When you become aware of it, your destiny code will reveal your unique identity, purpose, and path. It is a detailed picture of your potential.

Have you noticed how certain seemingly accidental experiences eventually connect with other random events and circumstances in your life to produce unforeseen benefits or spark unexpected desires? Often, aspects of these experiences repeat themselves for no apparent reason and are so seemingly unremarkable that they fail to register in your conscious thoughts.

Hints to your destiny code are often found in your relationships. Perhaps you have been encouraged in similar ways by a series of friends and acquaintances. Although they may or may not be connected with one another, they individually applaud a certain talent of yours or point out a unique quality which you may have overlooked. They might even put you in touch with other people who will prove to be instrumental to your success.

If you become alert to the signals these friends and acquaintances are sending and the patterns of your interaction with them, you will uncover aspects of your destiny code. These exchanges will become more meaningful and you'll realize that they are not coincidental. In a single revelatory moment, a sense of destiny can rush to the front of your mind. When it does, your dreams—whether new or resurrected—will command your attention in dynamic new ways.

Once your dream switch is flipped, you'll find yourself in sync with your destiny. Life's paradigms will begin to shift and you'll be motivated to make the specific adjustments that will facilitate your dream. Priorities will change, schedules will be rewritten, new relationships will form, and finances will be redirected. The events you once wondered about will become clear symbols of where your life is headed. When you become cognizant of the larger context of your circumstances, they will help you crack your destiny code!

Your destiny code can also be revealed in the things you love to do. Which activities, pursuits, or situations cause you to feel fully alive? Have you been writing poetry since childhood? Do stacks of saved notebooks document your otherwise unknown work? Perhaps you've moved across state, across country, and back again and realized that the only item that has traveled with you all that time is the tattered carton of notebooks with which you never could part. This could be a key to your destiny code.

Destiny codes can be revealed in the way you do things. There may be a certain pizzazz others recognize, perhaps your flair for decorating or hospitality. When friends consistently compliment your efforts or ask for your help with their projects, pause and take notice. They could be alerting you to your destiny code. Take their hint and follow through. You could find yourself riding a new wave of opportunity, excitement, and enjoyment in your life.

Your destiny code is as individual as your fingerprint. It has a rhythm all its own, a drumbeat only you can hear. It is nuanced and vibrant; it foreshadows the unfolding of your life and helps to frame your way of looking at things. Your destiny code influences the ways in which you articulate your perspective and causes your ideas to be consequential to others. Your destiny code reveals your inner workings; it shows just what makes you tick *and why.*

Your Destiny Code at Work

Whether or not you were consciously aware of its existence, your destiny code has been at work throughout your life. It is the reason behind many of the perplexing twists and turns in your path, even those you would like to forget. It has played a formative role in your maturation, often by way of events and circumstances that were uncomfortable or unwanted.

Have you ever heard the biblical story of Joseph? In his youth Joseph had dreams that foretold an amazing destiny. Not realizing the consequences he would face for sharing his excitement, Joseph described those dreams to his family. Because his dreams foretold Joseph's becoming greater than his brothers and because he was already his father's pet, Joseph's eleven brothers despised him. Some of them plotted to kill him. In the end they sold young Joseph as a slave and led their father to believe that he had been mauled to death by a wild animal.

Once in Egypt, Joseph served in the home of Potiphar, one of Pharaoh's officers. Potiphar's wife was attracted to Joseph and tried to seduce the young man. Faithful to his master and unwilling to commit adultery, Joseph refused her advances. Spurned, the officer's wife accused Joseph of having violated her. Enraged, Potiphar had Joseph thrown into prison.

What a dreadful sequence of events! Imagine the emotional pain Joseph endured; he was rejected and betrayed by his brothers, separated from his beloved father, and falsely accused and imprisoned for a crime he never committed. Yet Joseph's awful circumstances—and even the actions of his enemies—were a living, breathing part of his destiny code.

Through the associations he made in prison, Joseph became known for his ability to interpret dreams. One day Pharaoh, haunted by perplexing dreams of his own and frustrated with his sorcerers' failure to interpret them, was told of Joseph's gift.

Immediately, Pharaoh summoned Joseph to his palace. Joseph confidently interpreted Pharaoh's dreams and offered a solution to the famine those dreams foretold. Unlike Joseph's brothers who cruelly discarded him, Pharaoh quickly recognized Joseph's extraordinary qualities. In a dramatic turn of events, Pharaoh elevated Joseph to a high place in his government—second in command over the Egyptian empire!

Written into Joseph's destiny code was his rise to a place of influence and prosperity. His unique abilities enabled him to save not only Egypt, but his own family from famine. Although the winding path of his life seemed to move in a direction diametrically opposed to the dreams of his youth, the difficult passages of his life were no accident. They were coded with the DNA of his destiny. His slavery, sorrow, and imprisonment dovetailed with Joseph's patience and forbearance to cause Joseph to be the right person in the right place at the right time.

Your destiny code is working just as surely as Joseph's did. Much like a treasure map buried long ago and forgotten, your destiny code contains priceless information that, once discovered, will lead you in the direction of your dreams. It is not written on parchment, but encoded into the life you are already living. It unfolds incrementally and often speaks through the desires you cannot express in words. Your destiny code can be reflected in the simple choices you make and can attach to your decisions more significance than you might have imagined.

Consider the inauspicious beginnings of Ella Fitzgerald's life. The phenomenal acclaim and success she would achieve might not have seemed apparent in the days of Ella's youth. Almost certainly, the setbacks she suffered would have been seen not as promising and providential, but as downright demoralizing. Yet the day would come when a decision made in a single, nerve-wracking moment would turn the young woman's life around.

Shortly after Ella was born in Newport News, Virginia, her parents separated and Ella and her mother moved to Yonkers, New York. Tragically, while Ella was still in her teens, her mother died from injuries sustained in a car wreck, and Ella went to live with her aunt.

Discouraged by the dramatic changes that had been thrust upon her, Ella struggled at school, got into trouble with the law, and was sent to a reformatory. Ella managed to escape her confinement, but freedom from reform school equaled a life alone and without means in the midst of the Great Depression.

In 1934 Ella's circumstances began to shift when she entered a drawing and was chosen to compete in the famed Apollo Theater's amateur night. As Ella awaited her turn to perform, an unexpected circumstance complicated her plan. We can only imagine the range of emotions she experienced as the night unfolded:

> "Ella went to the theater that night planning to dance, but when the frenzied Edwards Sisters closed the main show, Ella changed her mind. 'They were the dancingest sisters around,' Ella said, and she felt her act would not compare.

Once on stage, faced with boos and murmurs of 'What's she going to do?' from the rowdy crowd, a scared and disheveled Ella made the last minute decision to sing. She asked the band to play Hoagy Carmichael's 'Judy,' a song she knew well because Connee Boswell's rendition of it was among [her mother's] favorites. Ella quickly quieted the audience, and by the song's end they were demanding an encore. She obliged and sang the flip side of the Boswell Sister's record, 'The Object of My Affections.'

"Off stage, and away from people she knew well, Ella was shy and reserved. She was self-conscious about her appearance, and for a while even doubted the extent of her abilities. On stage, however, Ella was surprised to find she had no fear. She felt at home in the spotlight."[2]

Ella Fitzgerald's circumstances, even the foreboding ones, worked in oddly harmonious ways and led to the fulfillment of her destiny. Her lineage, her mother's death, even the order in which the amateurs at the Apollo were scheduled to perform—played a role in the outstanding outcome of Ella's life. It is unlikely that Ella Fitzgerald was encouraged by the terrible losses she sustained in her youth. Yet as the passage of time revealed, every cloud in her life had a silver lining. The singer's destiny code had been at work all along.

The same is true in your life. Whether your name is Ella Fitzgerald, Bill Gates, or John or Jane Doe, your destiny code is continually running in the background of your life. If you will tap into it, the code will provide real-time guidance and direction for the longer term. It will fill in the puzzling blank spots in the developing mosaic of your life. And as you tune into your destiny code, you will become better equipped and increasingly motivated to cooperate with it.

If you search it out and embrace it, your destiny code will move you toward your destiny by helping you to:

1. Become aware and appreciative of your unique identity.

2. Know yourself more fully and be "knowable" to others.

3. Respect yourself and be respected by others.

4. Be motivated from within.

5. Recognize the events that facilitate your destiny.

6. Appreciate the roles of others, including your enemies.

7. Experience greater self-confidence.

8. Be celebrated by others on the merits of your authentic identity.

9. Appreciate where you are now and take life's challenges in stride.

10. Understand and fulfill your purpose.

Your destiny code is the DNA of your future. It contains information money cannot buy and will speak to you if you will stop and listen for it.

Crack the Code

You are surrounded by evidence of your destiny code, so why not take the time to uncover it! Begin by surveying the landscape of your life and digging beneath the surface of your experiences to find clues to your destiny code that may be hidden there.

Here's an example of an everyday person whose destiny code became more visible through a real-life situation. Consider her story and allow it jog your memory of parallel experiences in your own life.

> For twenty years, Kate worked for the same company and held the highest position available at the firm. She was adept and able to field any question. When challenges arose, Kate could be counted on to assess the situation and create a winning solution.
>
> Without warning the organization was dissolved. Kate's specific expertise, developed over two decades, suddenly lacked an outlet. With her job gone and finances dwindling, Kate was forced to consider new and unfamiliar opportunities that would stretch the limits of her comfort zone.
>
> In time, Kate accepted a position that required her to move across country. She was exposed to a different corporate culture and an unfamiliar job description. Kate's new position was a good fit, in part because it drew more directly on her

creative gifts. At the same time, it presented an unfamiliar set of challenges and required her to apply her primary skill set in innovative ways.

Kate was thankful for her new opportunity to shine. Yet there was no denying the difficulty of her adjustment. The loss of Kate's job upset the long-standing equilibrium of her life. She suffered an income interruption and was forced to move out of state, far from the support system of family and friends.

On the other hand, new circumstances increased Kate's ability to embrace change and provided an outlet for her creativity that helped develop her other strengths. In addition, her new responsibilities reconnected her with her lifelong dream to write a book, and her new business associations provided valuable connections in the publishing world.

Can you see how Kate's experience uncovered key elements of her destiny code? Although your experiences may differ from hers, you can probably relate to her experiences on some level.

Consider some episodes from your own life. Be open to seeing "old" stories in new ways. Suspend your preconceived judgments as to the positive or negative value of certain events and situations, and look for the silver lining that may be hidden within your clouds.

For example, if you suffered a broken engagement or some other setback, look beyond the obvious negatives and identify any blessings in disguise that arose from the ashes of your trauma. Then consider how these circumstances may be revealing of your destiny code. Write your thoughts down in a journal. Keep them in mind and remain alert to future opportunities to cooperate with your perfect destiny.

Destiny Codes and Your Unique Factor

No one paints like Georgia O'Keeffe. No one sings like Ella Fitzgerald. And no one does what you do the way you do it. In fact, there is an exquisite thread running through your life and it touches everything around you. Your "thread" has always been there. It is the one thing you are especially good at or best equipped to understand. It is at the very core of your destiny code, and when you allow it to operate freely in your life, it will open doors to the greatness that lies within you.

That something is your *unique factor.* When you recognize it, it will shed new light on your destiny code so that you can read it clearly and live the life you were created to live. Your unique factor is an integral part of you, always available and ready to be activated by you. At this very moment, your unique factor is resident within you. It is either being expressed or is awaiting expression in and through your life.

Your unique factor doesn't always look the way you'd like it to look. Even successful artists like Georgia O'Keeffe can be tempted to camouflage their eccentricities at first. Your unique factor is often the very thing to which you would prefer not to draw attention. What makes us unique can also cause us to feel as though we were sticking out from the crowd.

Yet the significance of your unique factor demands that you come to terms with it one way or the other. Whether by decision or default, you will determine to do one of two things:

> *Use your unique factor to your advantage (and for the benefit of others)*
>
> or
>
> *Defuse it (and allow the rewards of fulfillment to pass you by).*

Perhaps you are a design student and feel that your projects don't fit in with those of your classmates. Your instructors may even discount your designs or label your ideas as being too unconventional to be useful. Consider your instructors' input with care and respect. Have you overlooked functionality and created a design that only works on paper? Or have you brought something so new to the table that others need time to catch up to your innovation?

Be completely honest with yourself and then pursue your dream. Instead of fearing to stand out from the pack, put your uniqueness to work *for you.* The world's greatest designers, teachers, businesspeople, etc. are not followers, they are leaders. Yes they are open to dialogue and input from others; every great man or women values the advice of good mentors.

But in the end, they are willing to stand up to those who resist change for the wrong reasons. Regardless of the field of endeavor, each potential innovator comes to understand the value of his or her unique factor and realizes that it may be the very answer for which the world is waiting.

Your unique factor is often revealed in times of crisis or isolation. Anne Frank was a young Jewish girl who lived in hiding during the dark days of the Holocaust. Anne loved to write; she kept a diary, wrote short stories, and dreamed of becoming a journalist after the war. Anne's diary helped her cope with the stresses of being a Jew in danger of being captured or killed. She wrote these words in her diary: "The nicest part is being able to write down all my thoughts and feelings, otherwise I'd absolutely suffocate."[3]

Although Anne did not survive the Holocaust, her experiences brought a poignancy and power to her writing that is rarely seen at such a young age. Anne Frank's unique factor—her gift for the written word—flourished during a time of crisis and isolation. It continues to touch hearts to this day.

In the case of Joseph, discussed earlier, his unique factor, the ability to interpret dreams, caused him a great deal of pain in the earlier part of his life. Your experiences may be similar. You may feel rejected *because of* your unique factor. Yet if you honor your individuality and allow it to function freely despite your past experiences, you will benefit in the end—your unique factor will be key to the healthy development of your self-esteem.

When Joseph interpreted his own dreams and shared them with his brothers, they became angry. Their anger grew to the point that they were willing to destroy their own flesh and blood. Yet Joseph continued to interpret dreams. This very gift, once recognized by Pharaoh, set Joseph free and elevated him to an unprecedented level of success.

Once in power as Pharaoh's second in command, Joseph's many other abilities found expression. His wisdom, administrative gifts, and compassion began to work together and cause Joseph to be the fully productive human being he was destined to be. Can you imagine the positive impact of these events on Joseph's self-image?

Allow your unique factor to be the "advance team" that sings your praises ahead of you. Reap the benefits it offers and allow it to flourish freely. Your unique factor distinguishes you from the rest of the pack and empowers you to achieve the greatness for which you were created. It is an instrument always at your disposal. Use it wisely and employ it fully. It will leverage your other gifts, talents, abilities, and resources to unlock the door to your dream!

> *Your Authentic Identity.* This is your true self, the "real you" free of all masks, cover-ups, and false projections. Your authentic identity reveals your God-given uniqueness and underpins your God-given destiny.

Destiny Codes and Your Signature Presence

You have a style all your own. It is your personal brand image; it engages elements of your character and defines your behavior and conduct. Your style is recognizable by others and influences the ways in which they relate to you. Your style incorporates your unique factor and something else that is distinctively yours—your *signature presence.*

In Hollywood, signature presence might be considered synonymous with the "it factor," the indefinable *something* that makes a star a star. Although it is distinct from an entertainer's pure technical talent, the interplay between giftedness and signature presence can produce attraction to the entertainer at a visceral level. Even the most gifted performers have benefited from "it."

Frank Sinatra was one of those artists in whom signature presence and pure talent combined to produce bigger-than-life stardom. Few performers before or since have been celebrated the way Frank Sinatra has. His musical gift remains unquestioned. It was central to the development of his career, but his signature presence brought an added dimension to his art and his celebrity.

Sinatra fans will tell you that when "Ole Blue Eyes" took the stage, his signature presence could stop a clock. Sporting a simple black jacket, white pocket square, narrow tie, and an appealing nonchalance, he held court from a stool as only Sinatra could...and then proceeded to sing in his distinctively conversational style. Sinatra was one of the world's great vocalists, but his signature presence mingled with his talent to create a chemistry that could not be duplicated. He's one of a rare breed so universally acclaimed as to be called by a single name—*Sinatra*.

Signature presence plays a key role in political outcomes. In political circles, the word *charisma* is more apt to be mentioned in this vein. Political analysts, pollsters, advisors, and candidates understand the importance of charisma in wooing voters and they know it can make or break a candidate. With charisma, a politician can overcome seemingly insurmountable issues; without it, the brightest candidates in the field can fall by the wayside.

Signature presence operates outside the public arena. Whatever your lifestyle or profession, *you* have a signature presence. It is uniquely yours and has an effect on the outcomes you experience. Your signature presence impacts all of your relationships, whether professional, marital, or casual. Your signature presence is noticed by others and affects the ways in which they respond to you.

When your winning ways with people convey your love and respect for them, when your can-do attitude makes you indispensable, when your ability to smooth out relational wrinkles endears you or your cool head prevails when everyone else panics, when your integrity keeps you above the fray of petty issues, that's when your signature presence will draw attention and support the positive outcomes you desire. Your signature presence, like your unique factor, is part of you and reveals aspects of your destiny code.

Know Thyself

So, exactly who are you and what makes you tick? You may or may not be a renowned artist or a world-class singer. You certainly aren't next in line to a Pharaoh because they're all entombed. But you are *alive* and, believe it or not, the world is your oyster.

You are someone of immeasurable significance with an authentic identity perfectly crafted and intimately entwined with the destiny code that belongs to you and you alone. You are the one person on the planet who can crack that code and fulfill the destiny it reveals—a destiny that fits you like a glove, a destiny even the likes of Georgia O'Keeffe, Ella Fitzgerald, and Frank Sinatra could not have achieved.

To paraphrase Ms. O'Keeffe, you have things in your head that are not like what anyone has taught you. They are natural to your way of being and thinking and they are calling you forward to crack the code and embrace the wonderfully unusual person you are.

Turn the page; you're about to get to know yourself better—and you're going to love what you find.

3

TAKE YOUR STRATEGIC
LIFE INVENTORY

"Dumb ox." That's what his classmates called Saint Thomas Aquinas. Yet nearly 800 years after his death, the writings of Aquinas are among the most influential in religious and philosophical thought, and he continues to be one of the most widely read thinkers in the history of Christianity.

Thomas Aquinas' classmates misjudged him. His teacher Albertus Magnus did not. A brilliant scholar in his own right, Magnus searched out Aquinas' intellect. He engaged his student in academic discussion and experienced the young man's aptitudes firsthand. By taking inventory of Aquinas' intellectual gifts, Magnus developed a clear picture of his student's specific capacities. Therefore Magnus saw the potential others missed.

Armed with the truth about his star pupil, Magnus stood at his lectern and addressed the name-callers. He refuted their findings and set the record straight with these stunning words: "You call your brother Thomas a dumb ox; let me tell you that one day the whole world will listen to his bellowings."[1]

Magnus spoke with conviction because he had taken the time to investigate. He knew exactly what Thomas Aquinas brought to the table—and at some point, so did Aquinas. The young scholar learned where he fit and what he had been created to give. This knowledge of *self* helped him fulfill his destiny—despite ridicule or other obstacles in his path.

History proved Magnus right and history proved unequivocally that Aquinas was no dummy. Saint Thomas Aquinas brought his gifts, proficiencies, and passions (including his zeal for spiritual truth) to his field and achieved unquestioned greatness. In other words, Aquinas knew what he had to offer and he put his unique inventory to work.

Read the Label—Carefully

Although they studied with one of the world's great thinkers, the classmates of Thomas Aquinas failed to recognize his brilliance. They overlooked or misread his key ingredients, the very properties he would employ to make a mark on history.

The story could have turned out differently. If Aquinas had accepted the label of "dumb ox," he might have unwittingly surrendered. Imagine the impact: His landmark work *Summa Theologica* and other writings might never have been penned; entire streams of discourse might have gone undeveloped; and the history of religious and philosophical thought would have been diminished by the absence of Aquinas' influence.

With the benefit of hundreds of years of hindsight, we can easily recognize the implications of a destiny lost. Yet Aquinas did not have that luxury. As a student standing on the threshold of life, he had to search within himself—just as we do—to develop an awareness of his giftedness and understand its connection to his destiny. Without the affirmation and accolades history would shower upon his good name, Aquinas had to press into his dream and apply the gifts that would bring it to fulfillment.

As long as you live, your story will remain a work in progress. Like Aquinas in his lifetime, you don't have the benefit of your completed biography to help you figure out what your potential really is. Instead, you have to search it out, just as Aquinas and all great men and women have done.

Why is this point so important? The reason is simple, yet often over-looked: When you don't know what is inside of you—the dreams, abilities, even the unique way you are wired for a specific kind of success—you cannot and will not grasp the loss that would be suffered by letting it go to waste.

This loss is more than personal. It is not only experienced by those of us whose dreams go unfulfilled; it also impacts the unknown numbers of people who would have benefited from what we were created to accomplish or produce. The price of an unclaimed destiny is calculated in exponential terms.

Do you remember the classic film, *It's a Wonderful Life?* The story takes place on Christmas Eve as lead character George Bailey learns that funds are missing from the family savings and loan association. Faced with disgrace and certain ruin, Bailey becomes despondent. He decides to end his life because he believes that his family and everyone else in the town of Bedford Falls would be better off without him.

As Bailey prepares to jump from a snowy bridge into swirling, icy waters, his guardian angel intervenes. In order to reveal to Bailey the truth about his importance to the community and restore the broken man to his family and work, the angel shows Bailey what the world would have been like if he had never been born.

Through a series of flashbacks, the distraught man begins to realize the merits of his life and work. He learns that without funding from his savings and loan association, the vibrant town of Bedford Falls would have been known as Pottersville, a dismal town bearing the character of its cold-hearted namesake, Mr. Potter.

The flashbacks also remind George of his role in saving the life of his brother Harry after a sledding accident. Harry went on to become a decorated war hero credited with saving many lives in battle. George realized that if he had never been born, Harry could not have served his country or contributed to the saving of other precious lives.

Bailey had also helped avert a local tragedy. When a local druggist became grief-stricken over the death of his son, Bailey prevented him from accidentally poisoning a customer's child. George's actions saved the life of the innocent child and spared the druggist the professional, emotional, and financial devastation that would have resulted from such a fatality.

When he was perched on the bridge and prepared to die, George Bailey had lost sight of his positive qualities. His hasty inventory revealed only his mistakes and shortcomings. Racked with emotion, he labeled himself *Failure*. George Bailey misread the value of his life, that is, until the angel helped him see the "ingredients" more clearly.

Have you ever been unsure of your self-worth, confused about your future, or down on yourself because of mistakes and disappointments? Take heart, because you are standing on the precipice of a life-changing opportunity to find the answers you need. And you won't have to look far because the truth that is going to arm you for destiny is not somewhere "out there," but right inside you!

It's time to do what Magnus did, not for someone else, but for yourself. Get pen and paper and get ready to discover your God-given brilliance by taking inventory of the energy-producing qualities your dream generates, the core criteria, abilities, and values that empower you, and of five properties that describe the rich context of your life.

Recognize the Capacities Your Dream Generates

Your dream is more powerful than you know because it creates a quality of life that far surpasses dreamless living. For the next few pages, as you discover or rediscover the qualities wrapped inside you, stay focused on your assets, the positive features that will help you to achieve your dream.

Let's begin with the capacities your dream generates.

Your dream attunes you to destiny fulfillment. Your dream helps to keep your destiny-awareness active and fruitful. If you are a runner committed to winning a marathon, your dream will drive you to become particular about your conduct. You will avoid becoming sedentary and you will deny your inner couch potato. Your cupboards will be stocked with protein shake mix, whole wheat pasta, and power bars instead of chocolate-covered marshmallows and high-calorie baked goods. A dream pursued always affects your lifestyle.

TAKE INVENTORY: DOCUMENT SPECIFIC WAYS IN WHICH YOUR DREAM IS DRIVING YOUR LIFESTYLE. HOW IS THIS DRIVE CONTRIBUTING TO IMPROVED OUTCOMES?

Your dream focuses your perception and produces clear priorities. When you focus on your dream, your point of view and priorities become crystal clear. This elevates your level of motivation and improves productivity. The committed marathoner doesn't waste time wondering what to do and when to do it. This kind of athlete knows what it takes to get the job done without distraction.

 TAKE INVENTORY: RECOGNIZE AND APPLAUD THE ACTIVITIES AND PRACTICES THAT MOST CLEARLY REFLECT YOUR PRIORITIES. HOW HAS YOUR FOCUS BENEFITED OTHER AREAS OF YOUR LIFE?

Your dream directs your will. The runner's lifestyle reflects the dream of winning only to the extent that the runner's will is engaged. Discipline is never accidental. Getting out of bed at 4 A.M. will place a demand upon your willpower. Those who choose to live strategically take ownership of their dreams and are *willing* to make choices—even hard choices—in support of their destiny.

 TAKE INVENTORY: LIST THE WAYS IN WHICH YOU HAVE CULTIVATED THE WILLPOWER TO PURSUE YOUR DREAM IN EARNEST. HOW HAS YOUR SELF-CONFIDENCE GROWN AS A RESULT?

Your dream redirects your emotions. Most readers would agree that uncensored emotions tend to point us in the direction of our individual comfort zones. By nature, we prefer to seek immediate gratification, minimize sacrifice, and avoid opposition. But a dream can help us handle our emotions in more productive ways. For the aspiring marathon champion, the dream of winning will outweigh the desire to roll over and sleep in.

TAKE INVENTORY: CONSIDER THE WAYS IN WHICH YOUR DREAM HAS REDIRECTED YOUR EMOTIONS. HOW HAS IMPROVED SELF-CONTROL CONTRIBUTED TO THE DEVELOPMENT OF YOUR CHARACTER?

Your dream ignites your imagination and provides the vision needed to move forward. When you become actively engaged with your dream, it sparks innovative ideas, new thought patterns, and fresh perspectives. Your dream can illuminate your imagination and stimulate creativity in surprising ways.

During Lance Armstrong's years as a competitive cyclist, he and his team raised the bar in their sport. They put their minds to work along with their bodies and explored every aspect of the sport looking for ways to compete at a higher level. Lance, his teammates, and a team of engineers worked creatively to fine-tune equipment, enhance aerodynamics, and improve physical stamina. Their efforts produced an unprecedented record— seven *Tour de France* victories!

TAKE INVENTORY: EXAMINE THE WAYS IN WHICH YOUR DREAM HAS GENERATED INCREASED CREATIVITY. HOW ARE YOU AND/OR OTHERS BENEFITING FROM YOUR IDEAS?

Your dream affects your cognition. Your dream always seems "bigger" than your perceived ability to achieve it. Therefore when you take ownership of your dream, it expands your awareness of what is possible. Runners aspire to greatness in part because they believe that records are made to be broken. When you are "infected" with a dream, the question is no longer, *Is this possible?* Instead, the question becomes, *How can I achieve it, and how soon?*

Until Roger Bannister cracked the four-minute mile in 1954, most people believed it could not be done. Since then, three-time American Olympian Steve Scott has run the sub-four-minute mile no fewer than 136 times! Bannister, Scott, and others allowed their dreams to affect their cognition; they believed they could do what others considered to be impossible.

TAKE INVENTORY: CONSIDER THE WAYS IN WHICH YOUR DREAM HAS TRANSFORMED YOUR COGNITION. HOW HAVE NEW WAYS OF THINKING HELPED YOU RISE ABOVE OLD OBSTACLES AND EXCEED PREVIOUS STANDARDS?

Take Stock of Your Core Criteria

Your dream is jam-packed with power to produce *desire*, *intent*, and *passion*. These *core criteria* play an important role in positioning you to fulfill the purpose for which you were born. Your core criteria are not directed, not from external sources, but from inside.

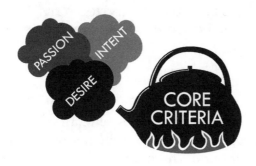

Desire. Your desires are meaningful to the extent that they are *your* desires. Desires driven by your authentic purpose are life-giving rather than life-draining. Your destiny code can speak to you through these desires even when your desires run so deeply as to defy expression in mere words.

Purpose-based desires are powerful instruments in the achievement of your destiny. Become consciously aware of them. Notice what stirs your emotions, even what makes you angry or frustrated. When you see an injured animal, do you feel compelled to help while others are content to stand by and watch? Compelling desires can be revealing of your purpose.

 TAKE INVENTORY: CATALOG YOUR MOST CONSISTENT AND PERSISTENT DESIRES. HOW HAVE THESE DESIRES MOTIVATED YOU TO IMPACT OTHERS FOR GOOD?

Intent. When acted upon, your intentions can contribute to positive life outcomes. We live strategically when we move beyond the point of desiring to do (or be, or have) something and become intentional about achieving it. Intentionality is the conscious direction of your efforts toward a specific goal or objective. Intention makes you willing to stretch to reach your goals.

Match your desires to practical ideas about how you intend to fulfill them. Always link your intentions to specific outcomes. Develop a sense of resolve that will keep you steady through life's ups and downs and propel you over any obstacles in your path.

 TAKE INVENTORY: NOTE THE AREAS IN WHICH YOU APPROACH LIFE WITH INTENTIONALITY. HOW HAVE YOUR OUTCOMES IN THESE AREAS SURPASSED YOUR RESULTS ELSEWHERE?

Passions. Each of us is passionate about something. These passions are seen in the activities that make us feel most alive, the conversations we find most engaging, the topics that lead to white-hot discussions with others, and the stories that stir our desires most profoundly. Your passions reveal facets of your destiny code and help fuel your determination to live your life to the full measure of your destiny.

 TAKE INVENTORY: REFLECT ON THE THINGS ABOUT WHICH YOU ARE MOST PASSIONATE. HOW HAS THIS PASSION PRODUCED INCREASED INITIATIVE?

Value Your Values and Appreciate Your Assets

According to *The American Heritage Dictionary*, values are " . . . principle[s], standard[s], or qualit[ies] considered worthwhile or desirable."[2] Your values are your deeply-held beliefs, the things you consider to be most important, and the things you are willing to live and die for.

Values are woven into the fabric of your identity. They give context to everything you do and say. They are reflected in your attitudes, they help you form decisions, they influence your outcomes, and they affect your relationships. Values are unwavering and enable you to navigate unfamiliar waters.

Values are the bedrock of your character. If you are an athlete who values honesty and integrity, you will not be tempted to cheat; if temptation calls, you will find the strength to resist it. You'll realize that when values are discarded or set aside for the sake of expediency, achievements ring hollow and victory fails to satisfy. Because your values are so fundamental to your identity, they are inextricably linked to the fulfillment of your destiny.

 TAKE INVENTORY: WHAT ARE THE TOP THREE VALUES GOVERNING YOUR LIFE AND HOW DO THESE VALUES HELP YOU PROSPER AND/OR BENEFIT OTHERS?

Some of our most essential assets are the ones we take for granted: the ability to *think,* the ability to *act,* the ability to *get results,* and our personal *equity* or human capital. The first one, the ability to think, is what separates us from the rest of creation. Our cognitive abilities enable us to stay in the game, even when disabilities or disadvantages become a challenge.

The ability to think gives rise to the ability to act—actions enable us to get results. Add to that the power of equity or human capital which is the synergy of your education and total life experience, your know-how, and your talents. The way you use your human capital determines the quality and the quantity of the material and psychological rewards you reap in the course of your life.

 TAKE INVENTORY: LIST SOME SPECIFIC EXAMPLES IN WHICH YOUR ABILITIES TO THINK, ACT, AND GET RESULTS HAVE COMBINED WITH YOUR HUMAN CAPITAL TO PRODUCE FAVORABLE OUTCOMES.

Imagine the power to realize your potential when these four key assets are mixed with your core criteria (your desire, intention, and passion), your values, and the qualities generated by your dream. But don't stop there—more good news is just ahead!

Your Life Space, Volume, Texture, Light, Shadow

You possess a depth of being known by no other species. You are a complex creation comprised of many interlocking elements—some that are familiar and some that might have escaped your notice until now.

Five overarching areas of life—we'll call them *properties*—encompass your unique way of thinking and being and lend context to your unique place, purpose, and destiny.

These five properties are your *life space, life volume, life texture, life light,* and *life shadow.* They can be shaped through your strategic life design, discussed at length in a later chapter. For now, let's explore these properties and inventory their impact upon your life.

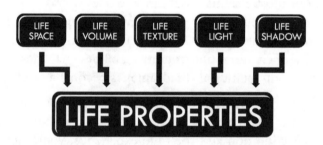

Life space. Your life space is the staging ground of your destiny. It includes your sphere of influence and your place of seizing opportunity. Although your circumstances change over time and your associations shift accordingly, you always have a life space.

Within your life space are the people you know. According to "The Law of 250" (widely attributed to world-famous car salesman and motivator Joe Girard), you know and are able to influence 250 people. These people can be found on your wedding invitation list, in your workplace, at the drycleaners, and in your home and community. Opportunity involves people so it is easy to imagine the dynamics that can be triggered when you put The Law of 250 to work.

When you fully occupy your life space through proactive, strategic living, your life space expands. It is a matter of "working" what you've got and maximizing every opportunity. Think of your life space the way financial wizard Warren Buffet thinks of his investment portfolio. At any given moment the value of his holdings is fixed, yet his potential to increase his wealth is open-ended. Warren Buffet maximizes opportunity by putting his investments to work. As a result his wealth continually grows.

It is obvious that although wealth protection is important to Warren Buffet, it is not his only priority. If it were he would bury his money in a vast underground vault. Instead, he works to preserve capital *and* produce yield. He does this by exploring the marketplace, interacting with the financial community, and seizing opportunities to drive his interests to full capacity.

Your life space is designed for full-capacity living. Living at full capacity requires you to unload self-limiting attitudes (including low self-esteem) and press past the arbitrary boundaries of the ever-beckoning comfort zone (the area in the center of your life space which is defined by the fear of failure). Comfort is incompatible with destiny fulfillment. When limited to the confines of your comfort zone you will:

- Fail to fully explore your life space

- Avoid experimentation and forfeit the power of your creativity

- Recede from taking responsibility for your life outcomes

- Forfeit the very opportunities that would have bolstered your self-confidence over time.

 TAKE INVENTORY: DESCRIBE YOUR LIFE SPACE AND THE OPPORTUNITIES IT HAS ALREADY AFFORDED YOU. WHAT ADDITIONAL OPPORTUNITIES CAN YOU DISCOVER IN YOUR LIFE SPACE?

Life volume. This is your capacity to contain and pour out what you have to others—knowledge, ideas, understanding, vitality, hope, giftedness, revelation, abundance, wisdom, potential, enthusiasm.

The sum total of your life volume amounts to all that you receive, *plus* all that you freely give to others. What you give to others is not subtracted from your life volume. Your life volume reaches its fullest measure when you refuse to hoard your bounty and instead share it so that others can achieve their dreams. What you help others achieve will happen for you.

We can share and expand our life volume in the course of our everyday activities and interactions, including through our:

- Relationships
- Professional and volunteer efforts
- Generosity
- Opportunities to mentor and encourage others
- Availability to others.

 TAKE INVENTORY: IN WHAT BENEFICIAL WAYS HAVE YOU PUT YOUR LIFE VOLUME TO GOOD USE? HOW HAVE YOUR EFFORTS EXPANDED YOUR LIFE VOLUME?

Life texture. Life texture describes the rich, multidimensional quality of life you were designed to live. Included in your life texture are four key qualities:

AUTHENTICITY—This quality reveals your willingness to be yourself, to be transparent, and to reject cover-ups. When you are authentic, you are accepting of your own identity and open to being known by others.

ACCESSIBILITY—In every interaction, we either add or subtract value from the life of another. When we are accessible, we touch people's lives in a positive manner and can identify our "touch points"—the unique ways in which we make enriching connections with others.

EMOTIONAL HONESTY—This is the ability to be genuinely empathetic, understanding, and compassionate toward others. Emotional honesty requires a level of vulnerability because in order to be emotionally honest you must run the risk of being hurt by someone you care about.

SENSITIVITY—This includes being respectful of the life space of others. To be sensitive to others means to be willing to approach people on their terms while honoring their feelings and being respectful of boundaries. It includes being others-centered rather than self-centered. Sensitive people experience favor with others and are often recruited as leaders.

TAKE INVENTORY: LIST YOUR MOST PRONOUNCED ASPECTS OF LIFE TEXTURE. HOW HAVE THEY ENHANCED YOUR RELATIONSHIPS IN PARTICULAR AND YOUR LIFE OUTCOMES OVERALL?

Life light. This is what others see when they are in your presence. It includes the way you carry yourself and the affect you have on others. Your life light is affected by your sense of self-worth because the "light" you reflect can never exceed the level of your perceived value. Because we cannot always detect our own life light, it is important to allow trusted friends and loved ones to provide affirmation *and* insight into potential growth areas.

TAKE INVENTORY: NAME SOME OF THE POSITIVE CHARACTERISTICS OTHERS SEE IN YOU. HOW HAVE ASPECTS OF YOUR LIFE LIGHT ENCOURAGED AND STRENGTHENED THEM?

Life shadow. Throughout this chapter, we've focused on our positive characteristics and become aware of the ways in which these characteristics support our life dreams and individual destinies. Life shadow is the exception in the sense that it deals with the darkened areas in our lives, regions where light is blocked and understanding is diminished.

Every living human being has areas of life shadow. These light stoppages include what are known as *blind spots*. Have you ever looked into your side view mirror before changing lanes on the highway and totally overlooked the Mack truck barreling your way? As enormous as a Mack truck might be, it can get lost in the blind spot where the angle of your mirror cannot pick it up.

Weaknesses and negative attitudes often hide in the emotional blind spots that develop when we fail to recognize or deal with our weaknesses and instead over-compensate by focusing on our strengths. In doing so, we bury our deficiencies and often lose sight of them altogether, preventing their exposure to light and healing.

As long as these weaknesses remain concealed, they will keep us from moving forward and hinder us from realizing our dreams. Signs of life shadow include:

- Defensiveness—The tendency to respond to criticism or attack (whether real or imagined) in an overly apprehensive way.

- Performance orientation—The attempt to compensate for low self-worth through perfectionism and high achievement in business, studies, and other activities.

- Recurring response patterns—Patterns revealed when we are triggered to respond to certain events, interactions, or situations in consistently negative or inappropriate ways.

Don't shy away from the discovery of your life shadow. Your willingness to examine these darkened areas can yield tremendous growth opportunities and take you to the next level in achieving your dream.

 TAKE INVENTORY: IDENTIFY ANY AREAS OF LIFE SHADOW AND DESCRIBE HOW THESE NEGATIVES CAN BECOME STEPPINGSTONES TO YOUR FUTURE.

Kudos to you! You've just explored a formidable list of strengths and developed the core of your strategic life inventory. You have armed yourself with a better picture of the many facets of your potential. Now you can use this picture to your advantage. Allow it to awaken an awareness of new opportunities and reawaken forgotten dreams.

Reflect on your inventory often, especially when you need to be reminded of how much you have to offer. A heightened awareness of your assets will dispel the false negatives that undermine self-image and limit life outcomes. And if that weren't enough reason to take your inventory, consider this: When you become familiar with your fortes and appreciative of their value, you will find unexpected ways to put your strengths to work.

This process of discovery is essential groundwork for the development of your strategic life plan. But don't park here. You're ready to clear the decks of unfinished business and get a clear picture of your *now*—next.

EMBRACE THE SEASONS OF YOUR LIFE

To everything, turn, turn, turn
There is a season, turn, turn, turn
And a time for every purpose,
under heaven —Pete Seeger, "Turn! Turn! Turn!"[1]

Life is a rollercoaster ride through changing seasons. Sudden turns jerk us this way and that, speeds pick up and slow down, we soar high and plunge low. As wild as the ride can be, life's seasons include the tranquil times we find easier to negotiate, places where we regain orientation and retool for whatever is next. In every case, whatever the season, it is a period of time that is consequential, formative, and essential.

With a career spanning seasons of cultural upheaval and social unrest, Pete Seeger witnessed life's twists and turns firsthand. With his fusion of modern music and ancient truths from the Book of Ecclesiastes, Seeger captured in "Turn! Turn! Turn!" the texture of life's winding ways. Universal in its message, the song was destined to become a classic; it has been recorded by everyone from The Byrds to Nina Simone.

If you're old enough to remember when "Turn! Turn! Turn!" was a hit song, you have lived its poignant message over and over again. But even if you're barely old enough to have weathered the woes of adolescence, you are already familiar with life's many surprises and messy transitions.

Puberty is one of life's quintessential seasons. Chances are it rocked your world, yet you don't regret having lived to talk about it. The physical transformation puberty produced has long-term consequences that are well worth the struggle. Still, you can probably remember moments that weren't pleasant. That's the nature of seasons: Over the long haul the benefits become evident, but the upside is often difficult to see while the transition is underway. When the monarch butterfly lays her eggs on the underside of a milkweed leaf, a series of transformations begins. The larvae feed on the leaf for approximately two weeks, by which time they become caterpillars. Soon each caterpillar finds a twig and attaches itself head downward. In a matter of hours, the caterpillar sheds its skin and is transformed into a jade-colored chrysalis. In two weeks' time, the chrysalis releases the monarch butterfly, one of nature's most glorious creatures. The monarch's unmistakable beauty is developed over a series of unappealing seasons.

Good Times, Not-So-Good Times

In life, our mountaintop experiences are easier to embrace than our trips to the valley. In the tough times when everything in your season seems to be working against you, finding the purpose hidden in the muddle can be counterintuitive at best. Nevertheless, the idea that there is *a season for everything and a time for every purpose* remains a valid one whose truth cannot be denied.

Life's seasons don't always seem to fit together. Yet even at their most disorderly and perplexing, they are a hallmark of life's design, the logical way in which life's journey unfolds. They add to our lives maturity, nuance, texture, and the element of surprise. Seasons keep us agile and responsive to changing circumstances. They discourage us from setting up camp beside stagnant waters. And when we're attentive, each season reveals new vistas of opportunity.

No two seasons are identical. Each one recalibrates our perspectives and elicits from us unique responses. The takeaway in every season—whether you would label it as being good, bad, or indifferent—is that it has destiny, purpose, and a new realm of possibility scripted within it. How much treasure you extract from each season has everything to do with the way in which you respond to it, whether with appreciation or disdain, desire or denial, reactivity or proactivity.

The seasons of life parallel those in nature. Nature's seasons give us clear clues to help us identify them. Those who live in the northeastern United States know that when maple leaves turn a dazzling, almost translucent shade of red-orange, winter's muted hues are following close behind. And for those who live in "Tornado Alley," the onset of spring with its troubled skies and rotating clouds revives the awareness of possible twisters ahead.

Life's seasons can't be tracked on Doppler radar, but you can develop the *savoir faire* to anticipate their onset and appreciate their purpose. Let's consider three principles that apply to all seasons. For each one, consider parallels you can draw to nature. Jot them down in the space provided. I've supplied an example and some hints to help you get started.

Each life season is unique in purpose and produces a "climate" conducive to personal growth and the achievement of that purpose.

Parallel: In nature, spring is the season of rebirth and revegetation. Warming temperatures and spring rains support these processes.

Life's seasons will change regardless of our participation or cooperation with their purpose. (Hint: How might the experience of a farmer demonstrate this principle?)

_____

_____

Life's past seasons are sealed in the annals of history. They cannot be changed, but they can continue to bear good fruit in the future. (Hint: How have natural disasters left their mark on society and how have they affected our commitment to preparedness?)

_____

_____

When you can detect the onset of a new season and are open to the new conditions each season creates, you become fully present to the moment and positioned to gain from times of change. Your season (regardless of *which* season it is) becomes a place of power and purpose, a place where you are geared to make an impact. This is significant because taking ownership of your season hastens the fulfillment of your dreams.

Seasons Are Linked to Your Destiny Code

There is an amusing anecdote about the time George Bernard Shaw and a companion attended the performance of an Italian string quartet. Shaw's friend spoke admiringly of the quartet saying, "These men have been playing together for twelve years." Shaw was not impressed and responded dryly, "Surely, we have been here longer than that."[2]

The seasons of our lives can affect us in much the same way as the performance of the string quartet affected Shaw; they sometimes fail to impress us and they often drag on longer than we would like. Yet each season—from the most fleeting to the (seemingly) never-ending—plays a role in moving us closer to the bull's-eye in the center of our destiny codes.

Although your destiny is encoded within you, the elements that facilitate destiny fulfillment—your gifts, talents, and abilities, your unique factor, signature presence, and other key ingredients—must ripen over the course of time. That course of time is marked by seasons and each one plays an integral role in the fulfillment of your dreams.

Physically speaking, it is clear that adolescence was encoded into our DNA for a purpose. Without this critical season of physical and sexual maturation, many of life's joys, including marriage, sex, and parenting, could not be realized. Without procreation, human extinction would be inevitable.

Yet the purpose of puberty is often overshadowed by the challenges we face in our teenage years. Many of us were beleaguered by embarrassing blemishes or alarmed by physical changes that made us painfully self-conscious. Some developed insecurities relating to perceptions of their attractiveness to the opposite sex and most of us experienced oscillating emotions over which we seemed to have little control. Even if your adolescence seemed as though it would never end, you can appreciate, with the benefit of hindsight, its overarching value.

When difficult seasons are behind us, it is easy to recognize just how destiny-connected they were. But this approach is *reactive;* it keeps us playing catch up. When we respond from *behind* the curve, we miss the key destiny moments and opportunities encoded in each season. There is a much more productive approach and that is to recognize each season and realize its vital connection to our destiny code, not as the season ends, but before it begins.

Become a Weather Detector

With every seasonal change in life, there are shifts in the weather, both externally (in your circumstances or relationships) and internally (in your feelings or in your changing needs and desires). Becoming a good weather detector will help you mine every morsel of destiny from each season you experience.

Good detectives are alert to the seasonal indicators that point to upcoming transitions. Let's explore some of these common signposts in the context of a workplace scenario. We'll examine four common climate changes: *closed doors, relational shifts, changing needs and desires,* and *feelings of constriction.*

CLOSED DOORS

RELATIONAL SHIFTS

CHANGING NEEDS/DESIRES

FEELING OF CONSTRICTION

SIGNS OF CHANGING SEASONS

Closed doors. Let's suppose that you have enjoyed an upward career track with a single company and are known as a go-to employee who always delivers. Your contribution, reliability, and skills have brought you favor with your supervisors so that when opportunities for promotion arise, your name is always at the top of the candidate list.

Suddenly you begin to sense a shift in momentum; inexplicably, your star is falling. No matter how well you perform, opportunities become fewer and farther between. You can see where you began and how far you've come, yet you can no longer see where you can go with this company.

Assuming your performance and relationships have not deteriorated through neglect, closed doors could be your cue that you're looking for opportunity in the wrong place, a place of the past. Closed doors can launch you forward into "now" territory.

Relational shifts. Suppose that a key relationship at work (one that has played a significant role in your success) has begun to wane although there has been no negative interaction and you are certain you have done nothing to precipitate the decline.

At the same time, another key player has taken you under his or her wing, for reasons that have not yet become apparent. This shift could be an indication that the former relationship has run its course in relation to your destiny. Meanwhile, the new relationship is coming into play; it will provide a platform for your next destiny step.

Changing needs and desires. There are seasons when everything on the job seems to be going your way, yet you feel empty inside and no longer find your work rewarding. You are able to perform with your eyes closed, the compensation is great, but you feel "flat" and uninspired.

Assuming you're not afflicted by depression, too easily bored, or fearful of success, this sense of lack could be alerting you to a change of season. It may be that you have given the company all you were created to give and received all that they had to offer. Nothing is broken, so there is nothing to fix. You need something more and in reaching for it, you will move in the direction of your destiny.

Feelings of constriction (or even disgust). This internal signpost is closely related to changes in your needs and desires. Suppose you've gone beyond the point where you feel uninspired and have arrived at the place where you feel imprisoned by your job. You realize that you are underachieving (even though others say you're doing a fantastic job). You live for the weekend and when Sunday comes, you develop a knot in your stomach. Assuming your feelings are not driven by an escapist mindset, they may be alerting you to the fact that your destiny code is leading you elsewhere.

Tapping into the connection between your destiny code and your seasons will clarify where you are and where you are headed. It will also eliminate unnecessary frustration and wasted time. Always check the weather; become an expert at indentifying transitions and check them carefully against your destiny code.

Become an All-Season Contender

If you'll become determined to take ownership of every season and deal with life's ups and downs in a positive manner, every circumstance will become an opportunity for victory.

Remember the story of Ella Fitzgerald's last-minute decision to drop her dance routine at the Apollo Theater amateur night and sing a song instead? As she watched the overpowering performance of the dance team that took the stage just before she did, Ella made an adjustment that sparked her illustrious career. She leveraged the hand she was dealt and achieved her destiny.

Every season gives you something to leverage. This includes *seasons of adversity.* Whether you have suffered a job loss, the death of a loved one, financial distress, or marital friction you can find something positive to be gained from the experience—a greater appreciation of every day lived, added wisdom in financial matters, increasing compassion for your mate— whatever it is, you can leverage your gains and improve your outcomes in future seasons.

If you're in a *season of crisis* in your health, business, or family, you have an opportunity to discover your strengths and overcome your fears. As you weather the storm, you'll gain the self-confidence to handle subsequent crises with even greater aplomb. Refining crises bring out the best in us; they develop our character and purify our motives.

We've talked about the sense of constriction that can signal a change in season. In *seasons of discomfort or limitation* you gain understanding as to where you are headed. You can see that you are being pulled out of something old and into something new that is aligned with your destiny. You can leverage this knowledge to release a growth spurt that will launch you to a new level in life.

Your ability to advance in every type of climate is dependent upon your willingness to focus on the positives in every season. If you are entering your most rewarding season to date but are prone to attitudes of fault-finding, unforgiveness, ingratitude, or laziness, you will fail to enjoy the beauty of the season and you will undermine its outcome.

Conversely, if you are in the throes of a difficult season but are determined to maintain a positive outlook—if you are gracious, forgiving, generous, thankful, and hopeful—your hard times will lead to unexpected triumphs and yield favor with those who are called to be supportive of your destiny.

When taking stock of the season you are in, remember that you are in a specific place and time for a reason—you are contending for your destiny! Avoid tunnel vision and refuse to view adverse circumstances with a magnifying glass. Instead, keep the big picture in view. Learn how to "see" what you do not yet have; as long as you can see your dream, you can move toward it.

Become Weather-Resistant

Seasons come and seasons go. You can learn to flow with the seasons without being overpowered by them. When stormy weather hits, you can fly above the clouds by becoming part of the solution. If you remain proactive, you will not be a victim but a playmaker in every season of life.

In each season, you have the opportunity to come into your own. In Chapter 2, we considered the life of Joseph who had been betrayed, sold into slavery, and imprisoned.

Under the most unfavorable conditions and despite persecution by others, Joseph excelled. In his season of adversity, Joseph came into his own. He maintained his high moral standards and remained true to his beliefs. He proved himself trustworthy and upheld his good name. He became wise and mature, a person who had a great deal to offer.

In each season, you are given a platform from which to create your future. While in prison, Joseph served his fellow inmates by using his gift of dream interpretation. Although he received no immediate benefits, Joseph's actions became his launching pad into freedom and power as Pharaoh's second in command!

In each season, you will encounter unexpected opportunities. Joseph's betrayal and years of slavery and imprisonment exposed unusual and unexpected doors of opportunity. These opportunities might not have seemed to line up with Joseph's early dreams of success. Yet he applied his talents wisely and remained productive in every season. Joseph's unexpected opportunities led to the fulfillment of his destiny.

In every season, you will have opportunities to bring transformation. Although Joseph's brothers were cruel and deserving of punishment, he remained forgiving and tenderhearted toward them. As a result, when famine struck, he was positioned to seize the opportunity to transform his broken family relationships and transform his own life.

In each season you can take stock and bring closure. In order for Joseph to succeed, he had to take stock of his bitter experiences, assess them in light of his destiny, and bring closure to the season of his betrayal. Had he not done so, emotional turmoil would have diverted his attention away from the opportunities that presented themselves during his years in Egypt.

> Clara Barton, founder of the *American Red Cross,* was not a woman given to the bearing of grudges. When a friend reminded Barton of a wrong she had suffered, the friend reportedly asked, "Don't you remember?" Barton replied in the negative, saying, "No. I distinctly remember forgetting that."[3]

Unload Unfinished Business

Seasons have the potential to strengthen, refine, educate, and advance us in the direction of our destinies. Seasons, especially the tumultuous ones, can also leave behind trails of unfinished business. Left untended and unresolved, these old issues cloud our perspective and keep us preoccupied with the past.

In Chapter 3, your strategic life inventory focused on your assets and positive features. You singled out your strengths and identified the ways in which these qualities support your dream. Now that you recognize your assets, it's time to take a second important inventory. This one involves unfinished business, the "baggage" we lug around from season to season, often without realizing it.

Unfinished business can be compared to spiny burrs that find their way under your skin. According to *The American Heritage Dictionary*, a burr is a "rough prickly husk or covering surrounding the seeds or fruits of plants such as the chestnut or the burdock; a plant producing such husks or coverings; a persistently clinging or nettlesome person or thing."[4] Burrs cause pain; they command your attention and siphon off the energy you need for constructive activities. You've probably heard the expression, "So and so has a burr under his saddle;" burrs attach themselves in the most inconvenient places.

Unfinished business is a burr that attaches itself at the emotional level and becomes an irritant so persistent as to obscure your vision of life's big picture. If you're saddled with burrs, you can't be fully present to the moment called *now*. And when *now* escapes you, your future suffers.

Unfinished business comes in many forms. Unhealthy or counterproductive attitudes including unforgiveness, victim mentality, hostility, self-centeredness, procrastination, low self-esteem, pessimism, passivity, fear, and timidity weigh us down emotionally and mitigate forward motion. These attitudes work against our interests and drain our vitality. You cannot develop a strategic approach to life or a strategic life plan when you are continually trying to fix an old problem or compensate for past experiences.

Blind spots, the attitudes and weaknesses we cannot see (but are evident to others), are another form of unfinished business. These blind spots, discussed in Chapter 3, are formed in our personal history, often in response to unmet needs. These empty places in our lives prompt us to chase affirmation and other emotional substitutes. They distort our worldview and affect our interactions. They keep us off balance and are often connected to other areas of unfinished business.

Misbeliefs can also keep us mired in the past. If you were told as a child that you were mentally deficient and unable to excel as other students, you may have built an entire fortress of beliefs around that single but potent untruth. Consider this progression of misbeliefs:

> *If I am unable to learn, then I cannot succeed in school.*
> *If I cannot succeed in school, then I am doomed to poverty.*

If I am doomed to poverty, then I cannot achieve my dreams.

If I cannot achieve my dreams, then I cannot overcome poverty.

Can you see how such a pattern of tangled beliefs forms a foundation of hopelessness and self-prophesied failure? As long as you remain in agreement with the lie you were told and the lies you bought into as a result, you will discount your destiny. Ironically, you will readily believe that others (those who are not mentally deficient, but may have other shortcomings) are destined to succeed.

Decide to inventory your unfinished business. Shake off the burrs that have attached themselves to your mind and heart. Refuse to allow these hindrances to clutter your mind. Don't be tricked into a perspective that keeps you off balance and aloof. Avoid approaching new opportunities with old paradigms that prophesy failure. Don't allow mere ideas to prohibit you from seizing real opportunities.

Clarity: The quality or state of being clear; it involves lucidity of thought and style. Clarity—about who you want to be, where you want to go, and how you plan to get there—is fostered when you tie off emotional loose ends.

Unfinished business will poison your clarity. It will cause you to mislabel your seasons. Without clarity your progress in life will be hindered and you will experience a diminished level of fulfillment and personal satisfaction. Lack of clarity will cause you to procrastinate. When your mind is cluttered with unfinished pieces of your past, you will unconsciously delay (perhaps indefinitely) the writing of your strategic life plan. You will be forever waiting for the day when you have your act together—and that day will never come.

Declare "The Season of De-clutter"

We have acknowledged the value of the past and of understanding its role in decoding our destinies. But when it comes to the clutter of unfinished business, the power held by the past is power usurped and wielded against the promise of your future. Read Herman Melville's indictment of the past:

> The Past is dead, and has no resurrection; but the Future is endowed with such a life, that it lives to us even in anticipation The Past is, in many things, the foe of mankind; the Future is, in all things, our friend. In the Past is no hope; The Future is both hope and fruition. The Past is the text-book of tyrants; the Future is the Bible of the Free. Those who are solely governed by the Past stand like Lot's wife, crystallized in the act of looking backward, and forever incapable of looking before.[5]

The clutter we carry from the past is no longer useful. It can be compared to a workspace in which nothing is ever thrown away. Imagine what your desk would look like if every document you ever handled and every pen you ever used was added to a growing stack of junk beside your computer monitor.

Eventually, the piles would consume your entire workspace. How much time would you waste moving the piles back and forth? And how long would it take you to find a working pen in the midst of all the dried out ones?

You would never dream of hanging onto all that trash. It would be exhausting and messy and you would eventually get tired of dealing with it. Yet, when it comes to the emotional clutter of unfinished business, we tend to tenaciously hang onto it. We allow it to obscure our vision, waste our time and energy, and keep us stuck in the past.

It's time to clear off your desk, empty out the closets, bring closure to your seasons, and restore clarity so that you can pursue your destiny with all the vigor at your disposal. Grab your pen and paper and use this simple list to detect any remnants of unfinished business that may be weighing you down:

1. Am I carrying a grudge against anyone who has wronged me?

2. Do I bear a sense of shame or inadequacy in any area of my life?

3. What things do I believe I am incapable of doing or of doing well? Are those things proven or have I simply accepted a lie as truth?

4. What unfounded or self-limiting fears have gone unchallenged in my life? (A few examples, the fear of speaking in public, the fear of making a mistake, the fear of commitment, etc.)

5. What blind spots may be fueling repeated missteps on the job or in my relationships?

6. What thoughts have crept into my thinking to convince me that I cannot achieve great things?

7. Which events in life have caused me to be overly defensive, fearful of change, or unwilling to take appropriate risks?

Back up the truck and haul away any junk keeping you imprisoned in the past. You weren't designed to lug around unfinished business; you are empowered to bring closure to it and cut it loose.

Take stock of the season you are in and get every last drop of goodness out of it. Tune into the signals that reveal the season ahead. You have an amazing life to live and a destiny to fulfill. Your future is bright and wonderful and you are uniquely equipped to design it strategically. Take the bull by the horns and turn the page. You have important outcomes to check out—both the ones you have already experienced and the ones you are still dreaming of.

> The past is ignorant of the present. Be careful in taking its advice.[6] —Mason Cooley

5

CHECK OUT YOUR OUTCOMES

"Surprise, surprise, surprise!" Famous words from Gomer Pyle and a fitting reaction to life's many unexpected outcomes. You know the drill. You put two socks in the dryer and only one comes out. Wear your best silk shirt and your chicken soup nails it. Marry the perfect man or woman and discover that no one can attain to perfection forever.

The outcomes we experience in life seem to have lives of their own and even the best of results can produce unexpected consequences. A whimsical story illuminates the lighter side of my point:

A man was driving down the freeway when he noticed a chicken running alongside his car. The man did a double take and checked his speedometer. "Holy cow! I'm doing 50 and I'm about to be outrun by a chicken!"

Dumbfounded, the driver sped up to 60 miles per hour, but the chicken continued to keep pace beside him. Not to be outdone, the man throttled up to 75. "This can't be!" he exclaimed as the feisty fowl passed him up. Finally, the man pressed the pedal to the metal and reached a blazing 100 miles per hour, leaving the chicken in his wake.

Satisfied with his accomplishment but baffled by his experience, the man looked in his rearview mirror and realized that his opponent was no ordinary bird. The lightning-fast chicken had three legs! The dubious man had never seen or even heard of a three-legged chicken, so he pulled off the freeway and followed the chicken home.

Finally man and bird arrived at a farm, but this was no ordinary farm. *All* the chickens on this farm had three legs! The man, thoroughly bewildered at this point, asked the farmer, "What's up with these three-legged chickens?"

The farmer replied, "Well, everybody loves chicken legs, so I figured if I could breed a three-legged bird, I could make some *real* money."

"Well, how do your three-legged birds taste?" the man asked.

The farmer looked down, tipped back his hat and said, "I don't know. I haven't caught one yet."

Poet Robert Burns said it succinctly more than 200 years ago: "The best laid schemes of Mice and Men oft go awry."[1] This paraphrased excerpt from his famous rhyme, "To a Mouse," is so familiar and so often quoted for a very good reason: everyone—including you, me, and the 3-legged chicken breeder—has experienced outcomes that didn't quite add up.

The Good, the Bad, and the Ugly

Much like the seasons of our lives, the outcomes we experience are varied and often unpredictable. But even though we can't control every outcome in life, we don't have to be sitting ducks. We are positioned to influence the results we experience and to respond to negative outcomes in ways that empower us to extract something good from *every* situation.

A real-life story speaks powerfully to this point and proves that even in our worst moments, we can make impactful, life-giving choices. During his heyday, long before he admitted to betting on baseball and long before allegations of other misdeeds were leveled against him, major league ballplayer Pete Rose went through a bitter and very public divorce.

As his marriage crumbled, Rose's wife aired her marital grievances in the press in devastating detail. Suddenly a chink had opened in Rose's sports-hero armor. Whether he was ready for the exposure or not, and regardless of whether he had it coming, Rose's private life was laid bare in the media almost daily. It was, in a word, ugly.

In the years since this unsavory episode, Pete Rose has earned himself many bitter outcomes. Yet in spite of his glaring imperfections and poor choices, he demonstrated during his season of marital woes a tenacity that is instructive: While the press focused on the scandal breaking in his life, Pete Rose dressed for games and kept his eyes focused on the baseball. During this difficult period, he excelled on the diamond and held a remarkable .311 batting average.

When a reporter asked him how he could hit over .300 in the midst of such turmoil in his personal life, Pete Rose answered matter-of-factly (his response is paraphrased as memory allows): "It's a whole lot easier going through a divorce batting .311 than batting .211."

What a striking statement, even from a guy who said, "I'd walk through hell in a gasoline suit to play baseball."[2] Pete's personal and professional failures are well-documented. Bad decisions and their consequences have tarnished his name and eclipsed his outstanding athletic accomplishments. Yet for all of his shortcomings, Pete's ability to *own* his career—the one thing he could control when all hell was breaking loose in his personal life—is commendable and instructive.

Pete Rose assessed the many variables he was juggling and sought to balance the equation. He understood what he could control or change (his athletic performance) and what he couldn't (the emotional fallout from a broken marriage and his own marital failings). The ability to make this distinction gave him a fixed point on which to focus when his ship of life hit rough seas.

That distinction—the choice to own our outcomes rather than be owned by them—is empowering in the extreme and never more helpful than in life's most difficult seasons.

Clarity at the Plate

"Hammerin'" Hank Aaron, who broke the all-time homerun record established by Babe Ruth in 1936, was a man who approached baseball with clear intent—to perform and perform well.

As Aaron stepped into the batter's box during the 1957 World Series, opposing catcher Yogi Berra noticed that Aaron's grip on the bat was incorrect. Berra offered Aaron some unwanted coaching saying, "Turn [the bat] around so you can see the trademark."

Aaron, whose batting average in the Series was .393, was undeterred from his objective. He remained focused on the mound and made his intentions clear, saying, "Didn't come up here to read. Came up here to hit."[3]

Become Clearly and Strongly Intentional

To assess our outcomes accurately, we have to compare them to our original intentions. First, let's refresh our understanding of intent and its role in the pursuit of destiny.

Remember that *intent* is one of the core criteria discussed in Chapter 3. There we defined intentionality as the conscious direction of one's efforts toward a specific goal or objective. This link between specific goals and clear, strong intent is vital. When we are clearly intentional, we are resolute and when we pursue our dreams with resolve, we are better able to achieve desired outcomes regardless of adversity.

Let's consider a basic illustration of the way intent works. We'll suppose that you plan to cross to the opposite side of a lake. This crossing of the lake is your intended strategic objective.

As with every strategic objective, your desire to cross the lake will require a sound tactical plan. To be successful, this plan must be based upon the conditions and other circumstances of the crossing, including the water's depth, the distance across the lake, prevailing currents, etc. These calculations will guide you in making decisions which are consistent with your desired outcome.

Let's assume that the water is deep and the distance across the lake is too great to make swimming across it practical. Since you clearly intend to cross the waters regardless of their depth and breadth, you will need a vessel suited to the situation.

After considering various types of watercraft, you decide that a rowboat is up to the task. However, if you choose to use a rowboat, you will also need an appropriate set of oars. Before you acquire this equipment, you must first consider whether you have sufficient strength to achieve your intended outcome—the crossing of the lake.

Assuming you have the boat, oars, and the necessary physical strength with which to row, you are ready to apply your carefully conceived tactical plan to achieve your strategic objective. You have combined clear intent, sound planning, an appropriately equipped vessel, and the required physical ability to achieve your goal. If all goes according to plan, these simple tools will take you where you want to go.

However, outcomes don't always turn out the way we hope they will. What if the currents change or an oar snaps or some other adverse circumstance arises? Assuming it is advisable to continue to the other side of the lake (recklessness is never a good choice!) and assuming that you started out with clear, strong intentions in this endeavor, you will want to realize the adversity you face sooner rather than later. This knowledge will position you to promptly evaluate the failure and make needed adjustments.

Because your intent was clear and your stance was proactive, your unexpected outcome will have moved you closer to success.

Close in on Your Outcome Gaps

With your understanding of intent in mind, you can deal with outcomes more effectively. When you are intentional, you are more inclined to own your outcomes, whatever they may be. This acceptance of personal responsibility (and therefore personal power) enables you to influence your results to your advantage.

In advance of your study of well-formed outcomes in relation to your strategic life plan, let's cover some of the common properties shared by all outcomes.

Outcomes are formed over time. Likewise, the improvement of outcomes is a process. It is important to appreciate this obvious but inconvenient truth: every outcome you experience will develop over time. Therefore, if you are determined to experience better outcomes in the future, you will need to accept the fact that the changes you desire may not be achieved instantly.

Pulitzer Prize winning American historian Arthur Schlesinger Jr. was quoted as saying, "[Television] has spread the habit of instant reaction and stimulated the hope of instant results."[4] Schlesinger's observation was astute; we've become used to seeing the beginning, middle, and end of a story transpire in one sitting. Somehow this "unreality" has affected our perspective in such a way that we expect the storylines of our lives to resolve just as speedily.

In contemporary vernacular, we might refer to this type of impatience as a *microwave mindset*. We want it *easy* and we want it *now*. We're uncomfortable with transitions and delays. We want to fix the messes in our lives quickly. But our expectations are often unreasonable; even if you can bake a potato in three minutes, the results you experience in life steep over time and can only be improved in the same manner—over time.

The American Heritage Dictionary defines a gap as "...A conspicuous difference or imbalance; a disparity...."[5] In general, gaps are perceived as incomplete or deficient areas, places where there are evident breaks in continuity.

Every undesirable or unexpected outcome reveals a gap between intended results and actual results. We'll call this discontinuity an *outcome gap* and define it as any disparity that exists between the results we intend and the outcomes we experience.

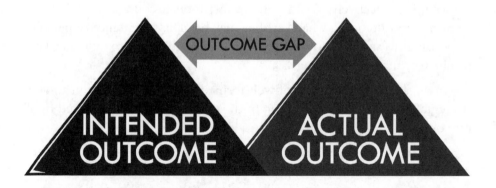

Let's keep in mind two caveats when applying our working definition of *outcome gap*. First we must realize that even under the most ideal conditions, the outcomes we experience almost never match our expectations perfectly. That is simply part of the human condition. Although it is important to accept this fact, this uncertainty should not inhibit our intentionality or limit our motivation to narrow the gaps in outcomes we experience.

The second caveat in regard to outcome gap is: There are times when the outcomes we experience result from of our *lack* of intent. Passivity rarely leads to results we would classify as being desirable. When unexpected outcomes occur because of our lack of participation, we feel the sting but often fail to recognize lack of intent as being the culprit.

In fact, because the posture of passivity is often hidden in an emotional blind spot, we sometimes go beyond the point of overlooking our personal culpability and instead seek to lay blame elsewhere.

Gaps between intentions and results develop for a variety of reasons. As you explore the following causes, consider them, whether by contrast or comparison, in the light of your own experiences.

PERFORMANCE GAP—This outcome gap involves the difference between our planned performance (the things we intended to do, the way we intended to do them, and the effectiveness we intended our actions to have) and our actual performance (the sum total of the actions actually taken).

Whether you have begun a new job, made a list of New Year's resolutions, or joined a health club, you are probably familiar with the challenge of living up to the performance goals you set for yourself.

Some performance gaps result from setting expectations too high. If you are a single mom with four young children, it is unlikely that you would be able to exercise at the gym for three hours each evening after work. In raising the bar that high, you will set yourself up for failure and the discouragement that goes with it. This negative outcome could deter you from entering into a more reasonable and successful plan in the future.

Performance gaps can also result from a lack of motivation, commitment, or self-discipline. Often we experience performance gaps when we have failed to count the cost of our endeavor ahead of time.

Renowned playwright Tennessee Williams engaged the services of a psychoanalyst, but abruptly discontinued the sessions. When he was asked why he had quit the program, Williams replied, "He [the psychoanalyst] was meddling too much in my private life."[6]

It is said that Williams had not intended his statement to be humorous, but the irony is apparent. Without an understanding of the client's personal issues, the psychoanalyst cannot facilitate resolution. Tennessee Williams obviously intended to reap some benefit from the psychoanalytic process, yet was put off by what he saw as an intrusion into his private affairs. Williams had not counted the cost ahead of time, therefore his intent was unclear. As a result, he was unprepared to endure the discomfort of emotional transparency in order to receive the gains he desired.

AWARENESS GAP—This outcome gap occurs when our intended results are compromised by a low state of awareness. In this half-awake state, key moments of opportunity escape our notice. We fail to take the right actions at the right time to produce the favorable results we desire, and we unwittingly put our dreams on hold.

When we are not fully present to the moment, open doors are overlooked and outcomes are sabotaged. Because these missed opportunities go unrecognized, they are often revealed only by the absence of longed-for progress or by outcomes that are less favorable than we'd hoped.

A low state of awareness can be caused by many factors, including:

Preoccupation with impaired self-image and unsettled relational concerns.

The presence of other forms of unfinished business, including blind spots (see Chapter 4).

Physical lethargy related to health issues or even a chronic lack of sleep.

If *anything* is preventing you from being fully aware and present to the moment, root it out—it's costing you more than you realize!

ATTITUDE GAP—Outcome "disconnects" can occur when counterproductive attitudes short-circuit your tactical approach to strategic objectives. These counterproductive attitudes can be promoted by distorted internal belief structures built upon misbeliefs, conflicting beliefs, and other untruths.

For example, if you are an aspiring singer, your beliefs about your vocal ability affect the level of success you achieve in the entertainment industry. Let's assume that you have, according to those in the know, a terrific voice and enormous potential.

Now let's assume that you instead adhere to the misbelief that other singers have reason to be more confident about their talent than you. When it comes time to audition for an important gig, your misbelief will factor into your performance and potentially undermine your results. Your misbelief will have become a self-fulfilling prophecy.

Conflicting beliefs can have a similar effect. Imagine for a moment that you desire to serve as a public official but believe, whether consciously or not, that others see you as being unattractive or unlikeable.

Based on this subjective assessment you will conclude at the subconscious level that you *cannot* succeed in the public arena. At the conscious level, however, you will continue to pursue your dream and state your intentions in accordance with that dream. Because you are at cross purposes with yourself, your conflicting beliefs will ultimately sabotage your outcomes.

Whether or not they are reconciled with truth, internal belief structures will always drive attitudes and behavior. And whether or not you are aware of what you really believe, your attitude will be communicated to others either verbally or nonverbally through body language, posture, eye movements, facial expressions, and tentative behaviors.

Look Back; Go Forward

When we carefully evaluate and learn from the outcomes we experience, we minimize future outcome gaps and prevent the perpetuation of cycles of failure and disappointment.

Conversely, if we choose to sweep undesirable outcomes under the rug, we will quickly discover that while our disappointments are hidden, they are never clearly out of mind. The memories we try to ignore become great piles of unfinished business which rob us of clarity and prohibit us from moving forward.

When it comes to surprises, know this: You are not alone. *Everyone* experiences unwanted results. The best response to these disappointments is to confront them head-on. Instead of beating yourself up, simply accept the fact that in life there is always room for improvement. Take ownership of the situation; assess the reality of your experiences and redirect your approach to achieve the outcomes you prefer. Consider this humorous anecdote from the life of legendary actress Sarah Bernhardt:

> An admirer of a certain young English performer was discussing her acting with Sarah Bernhardt, who was not at all convinced of the young woman's talent. "But surely," said the man, "you will at least admit that she has some wonderful moments." "Maybe, but also some terrible half-hours," countered Sarah.[7]

The hopeful actress critiqued by Sarah Bernhardt would certainly have preferred to impress the star. Yet even the unflattering assessment of someone as influential as Ms. Bernhardt would prove valuable if acted upon. I don't know how the young woman's career turned out, but it would have been in her best interest not to rationalize Bernhardt's observations as her admirer did, but instead to benefit from the input.

If we are skittish about constructive criticism or unwilling to admit that our tactics are not working as we'd hoped, we will hit the same old wall of frustration over and over again—and we will waste so much time repeating our mistakes that there won't be much time left to fulfill our destinies.

You already have the knowledge you need to examine a variety of outcome gaps related to performance, awareness, and attitude. This purposeful look backward is vital and leads us to develop the clear, strong intentions we need to move forward. That said, it is important to recognize two important truths about disappointing outcomes:

1. There are times when unexpected outcomes result, not from the gaps we've examined, but because the season for the desired outcome has not yet arrived. For example, if it is your dream to fly in NASA's space program, the realization of that outcome can only occur after you have been adequately trained and deemed sufficiently seasoned to deal with the physical and emotional stresses associated with space flight. To fly

before you are adequately prepared would be contrary to your best interests and could prove detrimental to the space program and to the safety of your fellow astronauts.

2. Bad outcomes, if approached with a teachable attitude, are never wasted. Do you remember the final outcome of the terrible rejection Joseph suffered at the hands of his brothers? Right—because they betrayed him, he was taken to Egypt as a slave. That's one of the worst outcomes I can imagine. Yet Egypt was the place of Joseph's purpose; it was where he would become the second most powerful man in the world. The seeming death of Joseph's youthful dreams proved to be the launch pad to his destiny!

Not all of the seeming gaps in our outcomes work against us and even when they do set us back for a time, they add to our character and strengthen us in ways that could not otherwise be achieved. If you'll grab hold of this truth and of the growth potential wrapped inside every disappointing outcome, you will leapfrog over obstacles and find yourself light-years closer to your dreams.

Well-Formed Outcomes

"Poor planning is the perfect pathway to panic" and "those who fail to plan, plan to fail." These axioms are well-worn because they are true. Planning puts us in the driver's seat in life by empowering us to establish goals and move toward them in a logical way.

Nobody wants to live from crisis to crisis and from setback to setback. Deep in our hearts, each of us strongly desires to live as those who overcome—not people, but the situations, attitudes, and circumstances that work to steal our dreams. For that desires to become reality, we need to first develop a clear sense of precisely what we want . . . *and what we don't want.*

Now that you've gained additional insight and perspective regarding the outcomes you've experienced so far, you know a great deal about what's working in your life and what isn't. But before you can develop a sound strategic life plan, you'll need to establish for yourself some specific *well-formed outcomes* and you'll need to express those desired outcomes in words.

What exactly is a well-formed outcome? Simply defined, it is the clear and comprehensive expression of a desired future result. We'll take a point-by-point approach to developing specific well-formed outcomes in a future chapter. For now let's lay some more groundwork for strategic life planning by exploring some of the keystones of well-formed outcomes.

A well-formed outcome describes and defines what you want to achieve. It is expressed in vivid, positive language that is personal and specific. Remember that our dreams of the future come alive in the present when we engage in a full sensory experience; that is, the envisioning of how your dream will taste, feel, smell, etc. (See Chapter 1.) A lack of specificity in goal formation could indicate an underlying lack of direction which, over time, will undermine your motivation, enthusiasm, and tactical approach.

A well-formed outcome includes an explanation of why you want to achieve it. Knowing why a goal is important is just as critical as knowing what the goal is. If you haven't explored or can't explain why you want something, your desire is either lacking a defined sense of purpose or is driven by motives which are suspect. If your motives are sound, identifying the *why* will anchor in your thinking the importance of the goal and help you stand firm in its pursuit.

A well-formed outcome delineates the terms and conditions under which you want to achieve it and is framed within a realistic life context. Remember the importance of counting the cost of an endeavor before you embark on its pursuit. You will need to ask yourself whether the costs and consequences of your desired outcome are acceptable before these expenditures are incurred. Related to these terms and conditions is the context within which your well-formed outcome should transpire. Determine whether a particular goal dovetails with other key areas of your life. Goals that don't work together will work against you.

A well-formed outcome includes consideration of all suitable approaches, addresses realistic timeframes, and considers whether key factors are in your control. By definition, a well-formed outcome is not vague. Therefore it requires exploration and delineation of viable approaches to the goal; it takes into consideration the time needed to accomplish the goal; and it necessitates the honest assessment of your ability to control the circumstances that are key to goal fulfillment. Without a practical plan for achieving your goals, your dream is confined to the "someday" realm of the theoretical.

Prepare for Launch

The development of well-formed outcomes is an important element in the design of your strategic life plan and a critical step closer to your dream. Why? Because these goals *speak* to your dream—they verbalize what you believe you are called to accomplish and they help keep your thought life focused on forward movement (and away from the distractions of the past). Well-formed outcomes give structure and vitality to your thought life, and your thought life directs your actions.

When you develop well-formed outcomes, you are scripting your future, not with a playbook that successfully controls every circumstance, but with a vision that will keep your life moving incrementally day by day in the direction of your destiny.

Whatever your current circumstances and regardless of the outcomes you have already experienced, your future has enormous potential—and that potential can launch you into wide-open territory that is primed for unlimited development.

The future is *yours*. Only you can design it. So prepare for launch—you're about to discover the power of the architect inside.

PART II

WRITE YOUR STRATEGIC LIFE PLAN

BUILD YOUR LIFE ON HIGHER GROUND

Every man is the architect of his own fortune.[1]
—Appius Claudius Caecus

The famous words of Appius Claudius were spoken by the Roman politician in defiance of Rome's enemies, but his words befit the man's character in a larger sense.

Although *Caecus,* meaning "blind," was added to his name when he lost his sight, Appius Claudius was a true visionary, a man famed for his innovation in public works. He is credited with the construction of the *Appian Way,* perhaps the most famous road in the world, a strategic link between Rome and Capua which enabled Roman troops and supplies to move freely. Appius Claudius also spearheaded the building of the *Aqua Appia,* Rome's first aqueduct, a high-security marvel and a feat of engineering at the time.

Appius Claudius may have been without sight, but he possessed a powerful sense of vision that elevated the level of his understanding and accomplishment and improved the lives of the Roman people. Like a master architect fixed on a mental blueprint of the future, he built Roman infrastructure with ideas and saw his ideas through to actualization.

That is the power of vision. It elevates your vantage point and empowers you to see what does not yet exist. With vision, you can rise above a business-as-usual mindset and approach life with a focus that is transformational.

Vision and the passion engendered by your vision will enable you to design your life from the inside out—from the place where your ideas originate to the physical world in which your dream becomes reality.

Become the Architect of Your Life

Blueprint

1. a process of photographic printing, used chiefly in copying architectural and mechanical drawings, which produces a white line on a blue background.

2. a print made by this process

3. a detailed outline or plan of action: *a blueprint for success.*[2]

That is what architects do. They envision what does not yet exist and see it standing on ground that is not yet prepared to support it. The architect brings the idea conceived from within and commits it to paper, first as a sketch and then in the form of a blueprint. The sketch portrays the idea in visual terms others can appreciate. The blueprint foretells in intricate detail the complete story of the structure yet to be erected.

"The architect must be a prophet . . . " said architect Frank Lloyd Wright.[3] Brilliant in his art, controversial and outspoken, Wright understood the role of the architect in setting the future in motion. He worked with intangibles, the power of his singular vision, and the elegance of his purposeful designs to create buildings that spoke in his unmistakable voice.

Frank Lloyd Wright grasped the breadth of his creative role. He knew that a great architect rises and falls, not on the strength of a single project or series of projects, but on the strength of an enduring vision. Wright's buildings are world renowned to this day. They continue to speak of his dream decades after his death.

Your dream does not rise or fall on the strength of a single accomplishment or series of events, either. Your destiny is fueled by an enduring vision, the ability to see the completed work of your life long before it is written in stone. That vision requires the support of a sound design, an elegant and purposeful life plan that ignites your passion, releases your gifts, benefits others, and transforms your vision into a desired end result.

A well-conceived design for your life requires the vision and expertise of an architect. That architect is *you*. No one can articulate your purpose and passion the way that you can. No one else has the ability to crack your destiny code and no one else can live it. Only you know or can know what you want out of life and only you can understand exactly why you are here.

Therefore, only you can design the life you will live. That design is far more significant than a blueprint for mere bricks and mortar; the design of your life communicates in visual terms the full expression of your destiny.

Vision Is the Currency of Your Life Design

When you uncork your dream, a compelling image of your desired outcome begins to form in your mind and heart. That image is your vision and it enables you to see the finish line (the fulfillment of your destiny) from the starting gate (or from wherever you are now). When you understand where you are headed, you can design your life the way an architect does, by working backward from the desired end result. In this way your blueprint will include all the elements needed to support the outcomes for which you are planning.

Your vision is a virtual document. It is interactive and unique because it is directly connected to your destiny code. Your vision is not static, but dynamic; it becomes clearer and stronger the more you are willing to yield to it. Your vision propels you forward and infuses you with new levels of enthusiasm and determination. Your vision will become so important to you that you will be driven like any good architect to commit your virtual document to paper. (This written record is your strategic life plan, the blueprint of your destiny, which you will develop in a later chapter.)

Your vision has intrinsic value. It is the energizing force that stamps your present with a prevailing belief in your future. It motivates you from within and instills desires that are compatible with the outcomes you wish to experience. Your vision promotes an atmosphere of innovation and causes your thought-life to be purposeful and productive. Vision is a vehicle that always drives in the direction of your destiny.

Your vision is catalytic. It works from the inside out to set in motion chains of events and courses of action that bring your destiny to fruition. Until you express it to others, your vision is hidden within your heart; yet it causes changes that are clearly visible. Your vision is transforming to self first, but when you are fully invested in your vision, its contents overflow the realm of your thoughts and seep into the domain of your actions, bringing transformation to the world around you.

Your vision provides guidance. You'll remember from Chapter 2 that your dream affects your imagination and ignites creativity. Vision gives you the guidance to train your brain so that your mindset is moving in the same direction as your dream. With your thoughts lined up (this includes your internal belief structures), your life circumstances can be reframed to support your life design and, therefore, the fulfillment of your destiny.

Make Way for a Solid Foundation

Being the architect of your life isn't just about building; typically it is also about tearing something down. If you've watched the evolution of a construction site from the beginning of the project to its completion, you know that before a new structure can be erected, an old one has to be emptied out and demolished.

Structures that meet the wrecking ball have simply outlived their usefulness. There was a time when they served their purpose and perhaps reflected the state of the art. But as the years passed, the once viable environments these buildings contained within their walls became untenable and new designs were sought.

In architecture times change, seasons pass, and designs become outdated to the point that they no longer meet the demands of modern function. As long as nonfunctional structures remain standing, progress is impeded. Until demolition is complete and the rubble is hauled away, the vision for something better remains on hold.

The same is true in life. What once worked well—whether comfortable routines, habitual ways of thinking, or familiar ways of doing things—may no longer serve your purpose. In order to meet the new demands framed by your vision, you may find that your life is in need of a new design.

You may have already laid to rest various forms of unfinished business. If not, you can start now. Once you've hauled away any emotional debris and any other structures that may be standing in your way, the next step is to prepare life's higher ground by elevating your perspective.

Elevate Your Perspective

Throughout human history, military strategists have recognized the importance of advantageous positions on higher ground. From hilltops and from watchtowers soldiers can survey the battlefield more effectively; they can track enemy movements, anticipate attacks, discover offensive opportunities, and design an up-to-the-minute battle plan.

An elevated perspective serves a similar purpose in life. Moving from life's lowlands where vision is obstructed to higher ground where the big picture is clear gives us a tactical advantage. It allows us to rise above the level of mundane to a place where vision directs our priorities and we can live in passionate pursuit of our destinies.

It is from this higher ground that we come to know definitively what it is that we want and what we don't. We become more discriminating and more specific; we rise above the level of wandering generalities and undefined purposes, and we create places of order where the path to destiny is clear.

To maintain an elevated perspective also means to focus on bigger, more consequential ideas and thoughts that are relevant to our destinies. At the same time, we become more keenly aware of what is essential to the achievement of our intended outcomes; therefore, we are better equipped to cast aside distractions.

Let's explore some of the qualities of an elevated perspective and the ways in which it helps us build our lives more strategically.

An elevated perspective will help you think big so that you can see past any obstacles and keep your eyes fixed on your vision. Try as you might to anticipate challenges, you will encounter unexpected obstacles on the way to your dream. An elevated perspective will keep these obstacles from overtaking your line of sight and enable you to see beyond whatever is blocking your path. In this way you will gain confidence in your ability to achieve your objectives and you will quickly bounce back from perceived setbacks.

An elevated perspective steers you clear of unfinished business and prevents the formation of new emotional burrs. Unfinished business is poison to the clarity you need in every season. When your perspective is elevated, you can rise above the level of the junk that causes discouragement. You'll develop a focus on your desired outcomes that is so clear that you won't be fazed by the grudges, shame, untruths, fears, attitudes, blind spots, beliefs, and memories that might otherwise attach themselves to your emotions and impede your progress.

An elevated perspective provides a clear view of opportunities to be seized and threats to be neutralized. Perched high above the "battlefield," you will promptly identify opportunities that are aligned with your intended outcomes and you will be positioned to seize these opportunities in a timely and strategic manner. This bird's-eye view also exposes any developing threats so that you can defuse them before they are successful in thwarting your mission.

BATTLEFIELD OF
OPPORTUNITIES & THREATS

ELEVATE YOUR PERSPECTIVE

An elevated perspective frees you to anticipate, innovate, and create. From an elevated vantage point, you are poised for proactivity and effective decision-making. Because your thought-life is freed from preoccupation with the mundane issues and distractions of life, you are positioned to respond to life in innovative and creative ways. Instead of applying temporary patches to lingering problems and making do with whatever is handy, you will create solutions and innovative strategies that complement your vision and move you forward.

An elevated perspective allows you to pave your way into the future and become a catalyst in the fulfillment of your destiny. Because your elevated perspective provides a view of the horizon (figuratively speaking), you can keep your future goals in sight. Therefore you are able to see your future not as something far away, but as something within reach.

An elevated perspective empowers you to give up what is good for what is best. When your sights are set high, you become intolerant of mediocrity and accepting of nothing less than what is best. You experience an increasing level of discomfort with lesser attitudes, abilities, pursuits, or results. This discomfort is necessary to the achievement of extraordinary outcomes and reminds you to drop self-defeating attitudes, wrongly motivated relationships, and counterproductive actions and activities.

An elevated perspective provides the encouragement and strength you need to accept the burden of your destiny (the fair price you will pay to achieve it) without moaning or complaining. Every dream includes a balance of burden and reward. To receive the reward is to bear the burden willingly and gracefully despite difficulty or inconvenience. An elevated perspective will help you stay focused on what really matters. From this vantage point, you will continue to see the burden as a blessing to be embraced rather than a curse to be resisted.

The Big Little Difference

"There is little difference in people, but that little difference makes a big difference. This little difference is attitude. The big difference is whether it is positive or negative."[4]
—Clement W. Stone

Elevate Your Attributes

You are a one-of-a-kind masterpiece equipped with a multitude of attributes designed for destiny fulfillment. You have a unique factor which sets you apart from everyone else and is only yours to give. You carry yourself in such a way that others recognize your signature presence and it trademarks your way of doing things.

Your life space is the staging ground of your destiny and your specific circle of influence. Your life volume is your capacity to contain life's bounty and to pour it out to others. Your life texture is your rich, multidimensional nature; it includes your authenticity, accessibility, emotional honesty, and sensitivity to others. Your life light includes what others see in you and how they are affected by being in your presence.

These assets and more are resident within you, yet they can only be maximized when they are working in unison with an elevated perspective and a clear life design. This orchestration of resources produces the most rewarding results.

For example, an elevated perspective and a clear life design work together in your life space to do two very important things:

1. The combination clarifies your view of the opportunities and threats surrounding you.

2. The synergy also reveals the significance of these opportunities and threats within the context of your dream.

Suddenly you can see the extent to which your life space is supercharged with possibility. At the same time, because you have the clarity which empowers you to move forward, you feel confident in your ability to preempt any negatives and rebound from any reversals.

Having a bird's-eye view and clear life design working together increases your life volume. This layered working of attributes ratchets up your ability to anticipate, innovate, and create and exponentially increases your capacity to absorb and contain all that you need to move forward relationally, professionally, socially, financially. Likewise your ability to share with others what you have gained will be enhanced.

Your life light will also shine brighter when you combine an elevated perspective with a smart life design. When your sights are set high, you are unlikely to drag around old, unfinished business. As your life light grows more intense, it provides illumination and inspiration for others. Interaction will be enriching to those with whom you are in relationship. You will also be a beneficiary of your life light, because what you do for others will be returned to you with interest.

Finally, try to imagine how your unique factor and signature presence will increase their impact when your elevated perspective and your well-defined life plan begin to work together, empowering you to believe and to behave in ways that reflect your destiny. How much more positive influence will you bring to every situation and opportunity in which you engage?

Your gifts, talents, abilities, and other attributes do not operate in a vacuum. Instead, they dovetail to produce steady progress toward your intended outcomes and to ensure the fulfillment of your purpose. The convergence of many attributes turbo-charges their impact and enables you to achieve much more than you ever believed possible.

A word about the "now" value of your many assets. Your gifts and abilities are designed for use. Saving them for a rainy day or a convenient time is akin to burying them in your backyard.

You've heard the axiom, *What you don't use you will lose.* In this application, procrastination in putting your assets to work will only delay (perhaps indefinitely!) the rewards that would have resulted from their activation. You wouldn't bury money in a mattress. Instead, if you have money to put aside, you put it to work for you. In the same way, don't postpone putting your gifts and other abilities to work. To do so is to lose valuable interest and forego the benefits that can accrue in your life account.

One more word about your assets—be willing to take risks to receive the rewards you desire. A reasonable level of risk aversion is useful, but if you don't risk *anything*, you won't gain *anything*, either.

Elevate Your Actions

Attitudes reflect perspective and drive behavior; the actions you take determine your results. The importance of this fact cannot be overstated, because your overall life experience can only rise to the level of your vantage point. If your thinking trends toward the negative (what Zig Ziglar and others call "stinking thinking"), your results will bear witness to your point of view. But when your perspective is elevated by your dream, you have an attitude that predisposes you to positive, elevated actions.

An elevated perspective will elevate the quality of your speech and cause you to verbalize positive ideas—about yourself, about others, and about the outcomes you expect. That kind of language is inspiring; it charges the atmosphere around you and generates belief in victory.

Have you ever been around someone who could light up a conversation and brighten your day with a few simple words? People like that are affirming, honest, and hopeful, even in difficult times. They are aware of the powerful impact their words can have, therefore they choose their words with care.

It is easy to see why these upbeat folks garner the favor of others. Their can-do attitudes and their generosity toward others have a way of rebounding to them in all the right ways. Whatever their technical gifts and abilities, it is their winning approach that sets them apart from the pack.

An elevated perspective affects not only your speech, but also the way you do things. Because you expect good things to happen, you take a front-burner, proactive approach to life. Winners can't help but act out what is in their hearts. They get things done because they attack their tasks with energy and because they possess an uncanny ability to focus on what's important. Regardless of how much is on their plate, they manage to do what is right, even when it is inconvenient—and they will do it for the right reasons.

Those whose actions are elevated by a winning perspective tend to prioritize well and act promptly. They are not prone to procrastination, in part because they do not approach their responsibilities with dread. They have counted the cost of their dreams and they accept the burden of that cost with gratitude. Therefore, they seize opportunities in a timely manner. They realize that every opportunity has an expiration date and every opportunity lost is costly.

When your perspective is elevated and your desires are attuned to your dream, your actions are undergirded with strong, healthy motives. You don't do things in a wishy-washy way. Instead, you take action with gusto and style. Your "want to" is evident and it attracts people of like mind to align themselves with you.

Your Want-To, How-To, and Chance-To

Your want-to is powerful; it can set off a series of chain reactions that lead to the completion of your dream. It's very simple:

Your want-to leads you to your how-to.

Your how-to leads you to your chance-to.

This combustion begins when you embrace your dream and accept with the full force of your intentions, the burden, or price, of your dream. This intense and purposeful want-to is directly tied to your destiny and it drives your capacity to be, to do, and to have whatever is necessary to fulfill your life's purpose.

Once you have a well-developed and well-supported want-to in your heart, the how-to will open up. Your want-to works like a magnet that draws you toward whatever you need to turn your desire into desired results. You'll find yourself associating with people who have the know-how you need. Learning venues will begin to open up.

In addition, because your perspective keeps you alert, you'll become aware of books, seminars, workshops, and software options that will fill in the gaps in your how-to. Other clues to your how-to will come from within; your growing ability to anticipate, innovate, and create will produce fresh new ways of achieving your desired outcomes.

With your want-to and your how-to at work, it's a matter of time before you will encounter your chance-to. Talk to anyone who is living their dream and they will tell you amazing stories about the chances that came their way at just the right time. I'm not suggesting that your chance-to will be handed to you on a silver platter. What I am saying is that when your want-to is aligned with your destiny and you become knowledgeable about the how-to of your dream, you will have immersed yourself dead center in the supercharged life space where your opportunities lie.

You can see that although this chain reaction is often seen as providential, it is by no means accidental. It presupposes the full and active engagement of a serious dreamer—someone who is committed not only to "arriving," but to the journey as well. Living your dream doesn't begin at your perceived endpoint (the unreal place where you feel as though all your ducks are in a row). If you are serious about the pursuit of your dream, then you are actively living your dream from the day you first embrace it.

Allow Your Future to Determine Your Present

Although the achievement of your dream may lie in your future, the dream and the journey that leads to its full expression are inseparable. Having the dream is critical; however, unless we take ownership of the journey, the dream will be lost. Consider the words of Joseph Jaworski, cofounder of the *Centre for Generative Leadership:*

> Most of us tend to avoid taking the journey to discover and serve our purpose. We refuse the call because deep down we know that to cooperate with fate brings not only great personal power, but great personal responsibility as well. When we do finally say yes to the call, we embark on a journey toward lifelong learning, meaning, and adventure.[5]

On this journey, every day counts. As long as you are breathing, you have the privilege to live the part of your dream that is called *today.* Don't lose sight of this truth; allow your dream to speak into your present and be prepared to listen. Make the best use of your journey and do with your dream what an architect does with a new building concept: See yourself standing inside it. Remind yourself to engage the full sensory experience of your dream daily. Imagine the way it will look, how it will sound, and how it will feel to live your dream. (See Chapter 1.)

Since your dream will not be comprised of mediocre outcomes, an "average" journey won't get you there. Discard any remnants of a ho-hum mindset. When tempted to think or perform by rote, push the *pause* button and recalibrate. Choose to think and perform in extraordinary ways. Find what is precious in every moment and every opportunity. Dig for your treasure if necessary.

Become increasingly intolerant of time-wasters and idle distractions and increasingly dedicated to elevated perspectives, attributes, and actions. Train your brain to focus on the unfolding of your destiny code and make decisions—about what you're willing to hear and say (and how you say it), and how you will act—in line with your destiny code.

Become so fit for your dream that you become *the difference that makes a difference.* In his book, *The Difference Maker,* John Maxwell tells the story of a young bride who lived in unpleasant quarters in order to be with her husband during his service in the U.S. Army. When her husband went on maneuvers, the woman became despondent and wrote home to her mother. Included in her mother's reply were these words:

> *Two men looked through prison bars;*
> *One saw mud, the other saw stars.*[6]

Although the circumstances did not change, the woman transformed the experience by adjusting her approach. On the strength of your dream, you can do the same in your world.

Finally, never leave your strategic high ground and never quit looking out of your watchtower because there is always an opportunity moving toward you. Start believing in outcomes you never thought possible. If your dream is vague, sharpen it to the point of high definition. If it is paltry, set your sights higher and dream big. You're the architect. Start sketching... and get ready to think outside the box.

THINK OUTSIDE THE BOX

If you've ever tried to solve the classic puzzle shown on the following page, you already know how the phrase *think outside the box* was coined. The idea of this classic brainteaser is to connect all nine dots without lifting your pencil off the paper. Solving the puzzle is easy enough, but only if you extend your line *outside the box*.

Voila! A popular adage is born, at least according to conventional wisdom. But *think outside the box* is more than a trendy phrase; it has become the anthem of innovators everywhere. From the boardroom to the boiler room, the way to shatter aging paradigms and supersede perceived limitations is to think outside the box!

Why is thinking outside the box important? Because there are things that just *can't* happen inside the box. The number of possible outcomes inside the box is limited. Metaphorically speaking, you've only got nine dots to work with and they are arranged in a rigid pattern that won't give.

However, *outside* the box, the realm of possibility expands exponentially. There's more room to maneuver, more ways to connect the dots. When you free yourself to think outside the box, you can turn your life's equations inside out, so that instead of just *solving* old problems you can *create* solutions, new realities that change the game altogether.

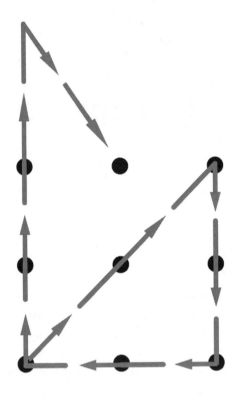

Outside the box you are free to think in ways that would astound veteran box-dwellers. Once you break out of the grid, you're in the company of people who believe that *nothing is impossible*. From the heights of that charged atmosphere, you can *create* your future with a single idea.

Become a Box Detector

Living outside the box is easier than ever. In a microwave, digital, on-line, globalized culture where real-time communication allows us to go anywhere at any time with the click of a button, it can be harder to stay inside the box than to break out of it. Still, if you've grown accustomed to the box, even in a single area of your life, you may not notice that it's there. That's where your box-detecting ability comes in.

You'll remember that in order to live a life that is supportive of dream fulfillment, you have to first recognize the dream and begin to envision, in the present, what you desire to have and accomplish in the future. That's the purpose of immersing yourself in the full sensory experience—the look, feel, sound, taste, and aroma—of your dream. By activating the sensory gates commonly known as your five senses, you can see yourself standing inside the life you, as architect, have designed.

To think outside the box, you've got to first identify and recognize that there *is* a box. Therein lays the rub: The box is often invisible to the familiar eye. It's been there so long and is supported by so many entrenched beliefs and formative experiences, that it becomes an accepted part of the scenery.

The box is like the thermostat that is awkwardly placed in the middle of a wall. When you first move in, the fixture sticks out like a sore thumb. Yet after awhile, you get so used to it being there that you no longer notice its intrusion.

That's the way the box works its magic. It blends into the background so well that you become comfortable with it. Before you know it, you buy into the security it offers without realizing the limitations it imposes. If you want to get free of the box, you need to become very intentional about detecting its charms. We'll explore four lures that make the box appealing.

The box looks familiar. The box contains everything you believe, know, and love. It is a stockpile of seeming treasures created over your lifetime. Not all of this cache is actually worth saving, yet it holds an emotional attachment for us; therefore, it has found a permanent home inside the box.

Included in this stash is your internal belief structure, which includes beliefs that are factually accurate and those that have been distorted (mis-beliefs, conflicting beliefs, and self-defeating mindsets). The box also contains choices and activities that have become routine. Among these are the excuses we make for situations we believe to be unalterable. The following chart provides some common examples of default behaviors and the rationalizations we use to support them.

DEFAULT BEHAVIOR	RATIONALIZATION (PARADIGM)
CODEPENDENCY	IF I DON'T TOLERATE THIS RELATIONSHIP, I WILL BE ALONE.
POOR EATING HABITS	I DON'T HAVE TIME TO EAT RIGHT.
POOR APPEARANCE	I CAN'T AFFORD TO DRESS WELL OR UPDATE MY HAIRSTYLE.
SEDENTARY LIFESTYLE	I WORK HARD. TELEVISION HELPS ME DECOMPRESS.

As long as you are willing to tolerate the contents of the box, your paradigms will remain uncontested and you will cling to the familiarity they provide.

The box feels comfortable. The box feels like a comfy pair of shoes: They may be out of style, but they are well broken in and easy on your feet. The box provides an apt retreat from the areas of life that make us uneasy, such as situations we feel unable to control or inadequate to engage. Inside the box our misgivings are assuaged; we become more desirous of a relaxing night on the sofa than an exciting night on the town. This is the comfort zone where all risks can be avoided—including the risks of failure and success.

The sounds inside the box are soothing. The box is never noisy. All you hear inside the box is the peaceful hum of the status quo. Differing opinions can be ignored here so there are no disturbing arguments or loud clashes. Nothing much happens inside the box so there are no blaring news announcements to disturb the peace. And inside the box, the sounds of protest are stilled and so are the rallying cries of opportunity.

The box is easy to touch. Once inside the box, everything you need to know and have is within arm's reach. The contents of the box are not elusive or ethereal, but tangible. Everything in the box has already been experienced; there's no room in the box for anything else. Therefore dreaming is unnecessary; in fact dreaming from inside the box is pointless.

You get the idea. Life in the box is small and easy to handle—too easy and too predictable to inspire a change for the better. When you consistently think inside the box, you are forced to recycle what is already there, including old trash, old news, and old outcomes. The more stale your life becomes, the more degraded your outcomes will be.

The box is nothing more than a coffin for your dreams. Inside-the-box thinking snuffs out vision and leaves in its wake the fear-clad *mis*belief that there is no way out.

Shell Crashers

Nature knows about breaking out of the box. When a female bird lays an egg, she keeps it warm and waits for the chick to peck and push its way out of the shell. Hatching is hard work, but unless the chick fights its way out, it will perish. And unless it succeeds on its own power, it will not gain the strength it needs to thrive outside its box.

Admit It—Your Dream Is Already Outside the Box

Everything that is in the box is familiar and time-tested. These are the things you already have, know, and believe. They don't inspire wonderment, curiosity, or sessions of soul searching. They just *are*. There's nothing left to prove inside the box; everything in there is common knowledge.

This is not true of your dream. Your dream has never been lived by anyone else. It is completely yours. You might recognize in history certain parallels to your dream, but it has no twin. It cannot be borrowed, mimicked, or photocopied. It is brand-new and awe-inspiring. Your dream raises questions, keeps you curious, challenges the things you believe and the things you take for granted.

Your dream is completely outside the box. There is no existing formula or preprinted label that can be applied to it. Everything attached to your dream is in the process of becoming—including the person you were born to be.

Until your destiny is fulfilled, your dream exists only in your imagination, which is perhaps the only place where your thoughts can form without restriction. Because the rules inside the box suppress unbounded inspiration, your imagination cannot function there. For your imagination to keep you in touch with your dream, you must follow it outside the box.

That bears repeating: *For your imagination to keep you in touch with your dream, you must follow it outside the box.* Your dream cannot be fulfilled inside the cozy confines of the box. Your dream demands that you reach for it. It will stretch you so far that you will be forced to release your grip on inside-the-box thinking.

Remember, when you have a clear vision for your life, it will seem bigger than life and beyond your ability to fulfill. Although you will see it with your mind's eye, you will question whether it is humanly possible to achieve. You may experience days when you are fully convinced that your vision speaks of outcomes that are impossible. But outside the box, nothing is impossible.

Outside-the-box thinking is a prerequisite for strategic living.

"Impossible" Is an Invitation

Innovative contemporary architect Daniel Libeskind has designed some of the most out-of-the-box structures in the world. When asked in an interview whether he had any advice for the young, he replied, "Follow the impossible."[1] Check out Libeskind's creations and you'll see that his advice is sound—at any age.

Become a Box Buster

Once you uncork your dream, you won't be able to cram it back into the box. Still, you will have to wrestle with the convenience of the status quo; every world-changer has. These are people who came to realize, in some cases via hindsight, that dreams are fulfilled outside the box. Consider the words of innovator Steve Jobs, cofounder and CEO of Apple, in a commencement address delivered at Stanford University in June 2005:

> Your time is limited, so don't waste it living someone else's life. Don't be trapped by dogma—which is living with the results of other people's thinking. Don't let the noise of others' opinions drown out your own inner voice. And most important, have the courage to follow your heart and intuition. They somehow already know what you truly want to become.[2]

Don't Get Boxed In.

In the most general sense, dogma is defined as "a settled or established opinion, belief, or principle."[3] Dogma is useful and important in the establishment of agreed-upon belief systems, as in the case of faith-based or political ideas. But if we become dogmatic about what is inside the box, we will inadvertently lock ourselves into the box and forbid ourselves the pursuit of destiny.

In his speech Jobs also shared what he called his "connect the dots" story. This is his out-of-the-box tale of how he found his purpose at age 20. That's when Jobs discovered his passion for innovation. But his epiphany didn't come in the conventional way. Instead, after his working-class parents had spent their life savings on the first six months of his college education, Jobs questioned whether it made sense for him to continue.

At the time Jobs had no idea where he was headed. Not wanting to waste any more of his parents' hard-earned money, Jobs dropped out of Reed College. Because of other aspects of his life story, his decision was completely out of the box and "scary" by his own account.

Jobs was uncertain how things would turn out, that is until he and his friend Steve Wozniak (cofounder of Apple) began a computer business in Jobs' parents' garage. The rest is history, but looking back Jobs can see how his "scary" decision to forego college ignited a chain reaction resulting in his phenomenal success.

Whether he realized it at the outset or not, Jobs had broken out of the box. From up in his watchtower, he assessed the big picture, questioned the status quo, and made a decision that set his destiny in motion. As a result he and Steve Wozniak completed three important destiny-fulfilling steps:

They found their purpose. When Jobs and Wozniak discovered their passion in Jobs's garage, they were on their way. It surely didn't look like much at first—just two young guys with an idea and not much history to support it. But they recognized their destiny codes and it was enough to get them started.

They framed it out. Once Jobs and Wozniak found their purpose, they pursued it wholeheartedly. They worked hard, even when all that was tangibly theirs was in the garage. Within nine years they created the Macintosh. A year later Apple was a $2 billion company with four thousand employees.[4]

They lived it out. Although Wozniak is no longer a full-time Apple contributor, both men continue to bring innovation to their field. Under Jobs, Apple remains on the cutting edge of technology; Apple products influence world culture and often define the state of the art.

Steve Jobs wasn't born with a unique box-busting, paradigm-smashing gene. He came to this world with a destiny code just like you and me. You were born to break out of the box, too. You've got your own watchtower. Your elevated perspective gives you a bird's-eye view of the big picture of your destiny. From the heights you can clearly see the downside of staying inside the box. Suddenly the box features you once found so alluring reveal their flipside:

Instead of a box that looks familiar, you see a box that is unfit for your dream. From your elevated perspective, you can see that the stuff you thought was important is obsolete; it doesn't fit with your vision.

Some of what is in your box is excess baggage and bits of unfinished business. It's clear that these items can only drag you down. Your transformed viewpoint requires that you *think* differently. Your old way of looking at the world seems small-minded now. And your old paradigm is unaccommodating of your dream.

Old routines seem pointless and old excuses no longer hold water. You'd rather own up to uncertainty and do what is in your heart, what is congruent with your destiny, than rationalize under achieving. You realize that everything is subject to change and change is not something to be feared, but embraced.

Instead of a box that feels comfortable, you see a box that is confining. From your elevated vantage point, the sofa is not as inviting as it once was. Instead of being a cozy retreat and a safe-haven from life's demands, your box seems restrictive. You feel claustrophobic when you're in it. It is clear that big dreams won't fit in the cramped quarters of your comfort zone. To stay there you would have to have your wings clipped when what you really want to do is to spread them. What once safeguarded you against risk, now clearly limits your access to reward, and instead of feeling protected from the burden of your dream, you realize that you are prevented from reaping its benefits.

Instead of a box that sounds safe, you see a box that cannot resonate with your dream. Suddenly the silence of the status quo is deafening. You long for the sound of life's hustle-bustle. You want to hear things that never seemed to matter before—even the clanging sounds of life's machinery and the dissonant sounds of conflict and innovation. You know now that in this cacophony is the melody of your dream.

Instead of a box that is easy to touch, you see a box that is keeping you out of touch with your destiny. You realize that anything worth having is worth reaching for and anything that can be gotten without having to stretch serves only to keep you from living the biggest life you can live. You're ready to appreciate the intangible elements of your dream, and you are ready to reach to the stars if necessary to fulfill your purpose in life.

With your dream at the apex of your focus, you see that, over time, paradigms are meant to be shattered. That's what progress is—the breaking of paradigms that have outlived their usefulness. Once your paradigm reaches obsolescence, it can do nothing but perpetuate old problems.

Determine today that you're going to bust out of the box. Acclimate yourself to your new altitude; pack on the extra red blood cells you need to sustain real living in the high country of your dreams. Condition yourself for an out-of-the-box lifestyle.

Ride the crest of your dream. Let it carry you forward. Defy the path of least resistance. Refuse to let your destiny slip away, because whether you bust out of the box or not, you will never get the dream out of your system.

You've already tasted the possibilities in your destiny code.

Fire the Gatekeeper

Every paradigm has a gatekeeper...and it can be found between your ears. That gatekeeper is your mind. In areas where your mind isn't enlightened by an elevated vantage point, it can be overly protective of the status quo and stubbornly resistant to change. Often a blind spot called *the fear of change* keeps this overwrought concern with paradigm salvation hidden from sight.

You can start box busting by exposing these walls to the light of day. Consider each of the following areas of your life and ask yourself whether there are any belief structures, habits, or routines that have outlived their usefulness and are keeping you inside the box.

1. Self-image (including appearance, self-confidence, personality), especially as it relates to characteristics you see as central to your dream fulfillment.

2. Level of education, especially as it relates your perceptions about qualification for your dream.

3. Communication skills, especially as it relates to working successfully with others.

4. Financial resources, especially in relation to your ability to pursue your dream.

Create Your Future

The shattering of unfruitful paradigms isn't just about tearing down. It's also about creating something that does not already exist. In Part III of this book, we'll uncover a wealth of information about how to move from the commonplace realm of solving problems into the stratospheric domain of creating solutions. For the moment, let's scratch the surface where this distinction intersects with our discussion of outside-the-box thinking.

There are times when dreams have gone unfulfilled for one reason: There seemed to be no venue in which the dream could play out. The story is told of a little girl born in the 1950s who wanted to be a priest. Instead of playing with dolls and plastic tea sets, the child created a make-believe altar on her parents' bed and re-enacted the rituals of Holy Communion. Wearing a towel in lieu of the alb and hoisting a colored cup in place of the chalice, the girl acted out her desire daily.

Her parents watched and wondered about the child's preoccupation with Holy Communion and asked her why she was pretending to be a priest.

The girl answered, "When I grow up, I am going to be a priest."

Unsure how to respond, the parents sought a gentle way to explain that, in their faith, only boys could be priests. The girl was stunned and suddenly understood why she had never seen a female priest in church. She pressed her parents with questions. In the end they convinced her that the priesthood was not an option for her.

This is not a statement about whether or not girls should be admitted to the priesthood. It is a declaration of this fact: *Regardless of the circumstances, every dream has a venue—even if the world doesn't know it yet!* If the venue for your dream is not evident at first, do not conclude that the dream is denied. Instead, realize that the venue is yet to be discovered.

Which is exactly the case in our story; in her adulthood, an unexpected series of events revealed to our subject a new reality. Out of that "created world" came a new venue and an opportunity to serve in another Christian "stream." The once little girl's destiny code had not lied; nor had she been baited into believing in a dream that would prove impossible. Instead, a series of destiny events led her to the time and place in which her dream would be fulfilled.

If the outlet for your dream is not apparent, don't quit on your dream. If you don't have a typical job description, then carve out a place for what you do. Create demand for what you have to give by creating your own sustainable advantage—the very feature that is so distinctive as to give you a competitive and unbeatable edge.

Do you have a home computer or even a laptop for use outside your home? In the 21st century, households with at least one computer are becoming the norm. Some families have one computer per child! But in 1977, Ken Olsen, the former president of *Digital Equipment Corporation,* said the following: "There is no reason for any individual to have a computer in his home."[5]

Tell that to Steve Jobs, Steve Wozniak, and Microsoft cofounders Bill Gates and Paul Allen. They saw the potential demand for home computers and software. They are in large part the reason so many of us own computers. They *created* the venue for their dreams. In doing so, they created their own futures and provided a benefit to society.

Your life story has that kind of potential, so get box bustin'! Break the mold. Respond to your current circumstances in new ways. Produce new outcomes. Reach for the stars. Create the venue for your dream.

Create your future.

8

COMMIT YOUR STRATEGIC LIFE PLAN TO PAPER

Each man should frame life so that at some future hour fact and his dreaming meet. —Victor Hugo[1]

In the realm of mortal existence, life is the main event, the context for everything else. It is no wonder that the definition of the word *life* as recorded in *The American Heritage Dictionary* is more than 600 words long.

From conception through death, natural life is marked by noteworthy events and a great deal of careful planning. Brides-to-be eagerly plan for their weddings, often spending a year or more to get all the details in place. Expectant parents study up on childbirth and rearrange their lives and homes to make way for baby—the most important addition to their lives.

Dreaming about life's blessed events and working to make those dreams come true are among life's greatest pleasures. Planning is *always* essential in producing desirable outcomes. The key to *strategic* planning is to not only plan for life's milestones, but to plan for the main event—life itself.

Your *strategic life plan* is the blueprint for your main event, and writing it down makes all the difference. You need a strategic life plan that will speak to you day in and day out, in good times and in bad—a plan that will encourage you and remind you that your dream is alive.

The only kind of plan that can do that kind of talking is one that has been *written* on a piece of paper.

Develop Your Mission Critical Statement

Your strategic life plan is rooted in your destiny code and at the center of your destiny code is the purpose for which you were created. Here is what Joseph Jaworski says regarding the role of purpose in fueling passion for destiny fulfillment:

> Many others have written about this need to discover our destiny or purpose. Author-psychiatrist Viktor Frankl says that the most basic need for any human being is 'the call of a potential meaning waiting to be fulfilled.' That call to meaning saved his life. When he arrived at Auschwitz, authorities confiscated a manuscript that he had devoted much of his life to preparing for publication. His desire to reconstruct the book enabled him to survive the horrors of the Nazi concentration camps. Frankl's experience led him to identify with Nietzche's insight that "he who has a *why* to live can bear almost any *how*."[2]

Your purpose—your *mission*—provides strength for strategic living. Therefore, having a sense of purpose and a clearly defined mission are fundamental to the achievement of your dream.

As you prepare to write your strategic life plan, consider your mission and be prepared to articulate in a succinct paragraph the purpose for which you were created, the values central to your purpose, and a description of the work you will do to achieve your mission. Your mission statement provides the headline; your strategic life plan will flesh out the particulars. *The American Red Cross* mission statement is a good example:

> The American Red Cross, a humanitarian organization led by volunteers and guided by its Congressional Charter and the Fundamental Principles of the International Red Cross Movement, will provide relief to victims of disasters and help people prevent, prepare for, and respond to emergencies.[3]

In their mission statement, *The American Red Cross* mentions the following:

The name of the organization.

The humanitarian nature and disaster-related purpose of the organization.

References to fundamental values as stated in other documents.

The specific needs to be addressed by the organization.

Whether or not you plan to create an organization, you have a purpose. Frame that purpose in a mission statement. It will power your strategic life plan.

Mine the Depths of Your Destiny Code

You were created as a matchless individual whose destiny code provides the direction necessary for destiny fulfillment. As you prepare to document your strategic life plan, reflect on earlier discussions regarding destiny code. If you haven't already done so, take the time to reflect on your life story and extract your destiny code from the following clues shown in the following figure.

CLUES	WHAT TO LOOK FOR
PROVIDENTIAL EVENTS AND CIRCUMSTANCES THAT HAVE PRODUCED UNFORESEEN BENEFITS AND SPARKED UNEXPECTED DESIRES	SERENDIPITOUS MOMENTS THAT TRIGGERED UNEXPECTED WINDFALL (PERSONAL, SPIRITUAL, FINANCIAL) OR AWAKENED A DEEP, DESTINY-RELATED DESIRE. ALSO TAKE NOTE OF THE SEEMING DISASTERS THAT LEAD TO SURPRISING TRIUMPHS.
SIGNIFICANT RELATIONSHIPS AND THE INPUT RECEIVED IN THE CONTEXT OF THOSE RELATIONSHIPS	INTERACTION, RECOGNITION, AND GUIDANCE REGARDING YOUR STRENGTHS AND EXPERTISE; CONNECTIONS FACILITATED BY OTHERS TO ADVANCE YOUR PROGRESS.
ACTIVITIES THAT STIR YOUR PASSION AND INFUSE YOU WITH ENERGY	THE 'ACTIVITIES' THAT TRANSPORT YOU TO THE 'ZONE' IN WHICH YOU FEEL FULLY ALIVE.
A CERTAIN 'KNACK' WHICH IS APPARENT	WHAT TO LOOK FOR: A SPECIAL FLAIR WHICH OTHERS CONSISTENTLY NOTICE AND DRAW UPON.
YOUR UNIQUE FACTOR	THE THINGS YOU DO OR UNDERSTAND ALMOST BETTER THAN ALMOST ANYONE ELSE.
YOUR SIGNATURE PRESENCE	ELEMENTS OF CHARACTER AND STYLE THAT MAKE YOU 'YOU' AND SUPPORT YOUR DESTINY CODE.

Keep Your Perspective High and Outside the Box

You're almost ready to start writing, but before you do, make certain your perspective is elevated. Now is the time to think big and see yourself soaring above life's everyday obstacles to achieve the extraordinary.

Finish up your unfinished business and leave it behind forever. Use your improved clarity to get a bird's-eye view of the opportunities to be seized and the threats to be mitigated.

Enlighten your decision-making process so that you can anticipate, innovate, and create in strategic and tactical ways. Prepare to write a strategic life plan that provides opportunities to pave your way into the future, inspires you to reject mediocrity in performance and outcomes, and empowers you to shoulder the burden, or cost, of your dream.

As you prepare to compose your strategic life plan, steer clear of the comfortable, familiar box described in Chapter 7. Rely upon your elevated perspective to help you see outside the box and into the vision of your destiny.

Pursue authenticity in the crafting of your strategic life plan so that it represents *your* dream and not someone else's. Remember, other people's dreams are already *inside* the box. You will have to get outside the box to articulate *your* unique vision. And because your destiny is always beyond your perceived ability to achieve it, your strategic life plan must also include goals that are outside the box—goals which require you to stretch and grow.

Before you begin writing, bear in mind that your strategic life plan will require your active participation. It must include specific, measurable objectives that will require you to override any passive tendencies and proactively pursue your dream. Passivity only works inside the box. Proactivity propels you outside your current boundaries.

Put every ounce of your elevated view and *outside-the-boxness* to work as you develop your strategic life plan.

Fine Tune Well-Formed Outcomes

If you've already checked out your outcomes, you have a working knowledge of any gaps between your intended outcomes and actual results.

Don't beat yourself over the head with evidence of shortfalls; instead, put this awareness to work in writing your strategic life plan.

Hone clear and strong intentions and put to work the other two elements of your core criteria—desire and passion. Remember that your strategic life plan deals with outcomes, and outcomes are produced over time. Avoid being impatient regarding timetables. Don't allow your need for speed to trump the quality of your life and the importance of your values.

Carefully craft well-formed outcomes (the desired results you seek to achieve) that reflect the pure desires that support your destiny code. Be precise: verbalize exactly what it is you want to do or have. Establish this "want" by simultaneously acknowledging what you do *not* want.

Also be able to describe the context within which these desires are to be addressed. For example, what burden seems reasonable and what costs would you classify as being prohibitive? How do you feel timing should be affected by other important concerns such as family and health issues?

Think outside the box and think big, but be thoughtful too. Recognize which factors are within your control and which goals can be reasonably pursued. For instance, if you are under five feet tall and not passionate about basketball, don't spend your life trying to become an NBA star center just because it looks exciting. The example is extreme, but you get the idea.

Be sensitive to timing as well. Let's assume that you are expecting twins this year and have always dreamed of being a restaurateur. Carefully consider your priorities and your stamina before you decide when to open your first restaurant. This year might not be the best time for such a formidable undertaking. You want to *achieve* your goals, not create unattainable or unreasonable aspirations.

Your well-formed outcomes should include a level of measurability. This means that you should be able at any given point to recognize whether or not you are progressing toward your goals. If you dream of becoming a surgeon, establish in advance the landmarks that will substantiate your progress. Successful completion of your bachelor's degree, acceptance into medical school, completion of your internship and residency, success in completion of any specialty training, and the attainment of certification are measurable objectives that track progress.

Pony Up Your Assets

William Wordsworth, one of the world's greatest poets, reportedly bragged about his giftedness within earshot of fellow writer Charles Lamb, saying, "I could write Shakespeare if I had a mind to." Lamb replied acerbically, "So it's only the mind that's lacking."[4]

In its humorous way, the story raises the issue of the subtle identity confusion experienced by so many people in relation to their unique purpose and giftedness. Wordsworth was brilliant in his own right. With the benefit of hindsight, it is clear that his destiny was to leave the literary legacy of Wordsworth; the world didn't need another Shakespeare!

Your strategic life inventory from Chapter 3 provides a well-rounded picture of the gifts, abilities, and other attributes you bring to the table. It highlights the beauty of your individual makeup and mission. It is linked back to your destiny code in the sense that your attributes are not accidental, but indicative of your life's purpose.

Besides providing clues to your destiny code, your unique qualities are the tools that make you more effective and well-suited to your purpose than anyone else. Everything from your ability to think to your specific life space factors into the completion of your mission.

In Chapter 6, we talked about the way your many attributes dovetail, enabling you to progress toward your desired outcomes and the fulfillment of your purpose. This *gift convergence* is the intersection of your destiny assets, the place where your abilities interact so as to yield greater results.

You may see yourself as being a jack of all trades and master of none. Your interests and abilities may seem senselessly divergent and lacking in cohesion. Yet the layering of your attributes is precisely geared to destiny fulfillment. Once you acknowledge this dynamic and allow it to flourish, you will begin to see how your attributes flow together rather than apart.

Your attributes help shape your strategic life plan. At the same time, your strategic life plan molds your attributes. Carefully consider your assets as you develop your strategic life plan. In this way your gift convergence will find its fullest expression and your strategic life will produce its greatest impact.

Strategic Belief: I Can and I Will

Your strategic life plan will articulate a future that does not yet exist. To attain to something that can only be seen in your mind and heart, you must *believe* in it and in your role in bringing it about. It is not a matter of wishing and hoping; it is a matter of desiring and taking responsibility for a series of well-formed outcomes.

At any given moment, you believe *something* about *everything* of which you are aware. Let's assume that you are preparing to take your bar exam. Whether you are consciously aware of it or not (and I urge you to develop this level of awareness), you either believe you can pass the exam or you believe that you cannot.

Either way your belief is an expression of faith in a particular outcome. This is important because each way of believing produces a distinct outcome. Faith in a positive outcome will inspire proactivity in pursuit of that result. On the other hand, faith that you cannot pass the exam requires nothing more of you; you can achieve failure by doing nothing.

That's where intentionality comes in. No one can expect to live their life's dream by sitting passively by and *hoping* for the right future to show up. Your strategic life plan must rest on clear, strong intent and the belief that you can and will fulfill your destiny—that you can and will make a difference.

Value the Qualities of Your Strategic Life Plan

Your strategic life plan is a multi-faceted, dynamic document with which you can interact over time to produce the outcomes it foretells. Before you begin writing, let's look at some of the qualities of your strategic life plan.

It is a document of solutions. Your strategic life plan matches well-formed outcomes to sound strategies and tactics designed to achieve those outcomes. It does for your life what the architect's blueprint does for a building: It brings the vision so clearly into focus as to facilitate its manifestation in the physical world. Your strategic life plan will serve to close outcome gaps and engender integrity, not by inspiring rigid behaviors and impossible standards, but by promoting dynamic inquiry into outcome gaps already experienced.

It is a motivating document. As you write your strategic life plan, you will assimilate it into your consciousness. The document will help you maintain an elevated perspective. It will instill confidence and remind you that you are not alone in this plan because your strategic life plan involves and affects others. Your strategic life plan will also help you assess and manage risk because potential downsides will always be measured against your desired rewards.

It provides guidance and a sense of priority. Your strategic life plan will help you steer toward life's best outcomes and away from lesser, more convenient goals. Your strategic life plan will also help you avoid rabbit trails; it will highlight your priorities and help you maintain focus. Once it is written, you can use your strategic life plan as a destiny-calibrated GPS device that can keep you from getting lost in the wilderness of life's conflicting demands.

Consider Your Future, Your Legacy, and Your Enriched Life

Before you begin writing, you'll want to consider important factors that weigh into your strategic life plan. Among these is the concept of *your desired future* and what it will look like. Remember, you have to see the end from the beginning in order to arrive at your intended destination.

You'll also want to consider *your legacy*. This includes your achievements (including benefits to others, innovations, and the establishment of ongoing organizations) as well as the example you set en route to your achievements. Your legacy will also be impacted by your sense of generativity which is the commitment to those outside your most significant relationships—to family, society, and future generations. Your legacy will also include positive, unexpected side effects of your fulfilled purpose. Consider these to be the overflow of your strategic life.

A strategic approach engages all areas of life. The third area you'll want to consider relates to *wealth-building*. This is not limited to the realm of financial gain, but extends to your spiritual and social development and well-being. Your strategic life plan should state your intent to grow in these areas and include methods and goals designed to precipitate your intended outcomes.

Consider Feasibility, Cost, Function, and Aesthetics

Feasible

1. Capable of being accomplished or brought about; possible: *a feasible plan.*

2. Used or dealt with successfully; suitable: *feasible new sources of energy.*

3. Logical; likely: *a feasible explanation.*[5]

In relation to your strategic life plan, you are both *architect* and *occupant.* As architect, you are the builder of your strategic life. Your creativity is matched with your purpose so you are best equipped to design your life.

However, you are also the occupant or user of your strategic life plan. These are the hats you wear as it relates to your strategic life plan. Each one focuses your attention on different features of your plan. Let's first consider two features that concern you as architect. These are the *feasibility* of your plan and the *cost* of its fulfillment.

Feasibility. Before a building plan can be wisely set in motion, the architect will require a feasibility study. This study establishes well-considered parameters as to what is possible and what can be successful.

In designing your strategic life, your feasibility study should include a comprehensive appraisal of your gifts, an understanding of your gift convergence, and an appreciation of your strengths. You will also want to be aware of those areas in which you will need to partner with others to achieve your desired outcomes. In addition, your feasibility study should include an assessment of the opportunities and threats you currently face or are likely to encounter.

cost

The expenditure of something, such as time or labor, necessary for the attainment of a goal.[6]

Cost. Before you can commit to any project or aspiration, you must assess the cost of completion. In regard to your strategic life plan, the cost is expressed not only in terms of any required financial outlay, but also in terms of the sacrifice, or burden, involved in fulfilling one's destiny. Your strategic life plan should clearly define the costs, delineate the available resources and future means of paying those costs, and establish your unmitigated commitment to pay the price of your dream.

> function
>
> The action for which a person or thing is particularly fitted or employed.[7]

Now it's time to put on your user hat in regard to your strategic life plan. Let's consider two factors of the plan that warrant your attention as a user: They are *function* and *aesthetics.*

Function. As the user of your strategic life plan, you'll want to ensure that the purpose and intent of the plan are aligned with your ultimate objectives. This requires that you become cognizant of your life's purpose. When your plan is functional and linked with your purpose, it is positioned to produce rewards in keeping with your established intent.

For our purposes, aesthetics involves the perception of what is beautiful and pleasing to the senses, as revealed in appearance and through experience.

Aesthetics. As the user of your strategic life plan, you are not concerned only with the mechanics of the plan. You are also interested in the ability to enjoy your plan. Therefore it is important to craft a plan that is in keeping with your aesthetic values. Don't be ashamed to state your desired outcomes; declare them with clarity. Remember that when you are focused on your authentic purpose, your desires will be appropriate. A strategic life design that does not encompass the pleasures involved in the pursuit of your dream will be an unattractive plan and therefore, less likely to be effective.

Start Writing!

Now is the time to put the power of your creativity and intent to work in writing your strategic life plan. Before ink hits the page, bear in mind three necessary qualities of a well-designed strategic life plan:

1. Firmness—your plan should be fixed in place, certain in its approach, and resilient in the face of challenges.

2. Usefulness—because your plan is linked to your purpose, it should add value to the life of everyone it touches.

3. Delight—your plan should promote satisfaction and joy for all who are involved in or affected by its fulfillment.

Your strategic life plan is a comprehensive document, a kind of life map which summarizes your life design in an orderly fashion. It is broad enough to capture the big picture and detailed enough to be relevant, timely, and useful throughout the ongoing pursuit of your destiny. Your strategic life plan can also delineate goals to be achieved in the lifetimes of subsequent generations.

Clear Vision

Creating a world where no American fears cancer.[8]

The *American Cancer Society's* vision statement is only eight words long, but it clearly and powerfully states the vision of the organization.

You can design your strategic life plan in a format that works best for you; however, certain fundamental elements are necessary. These include the following:

A clear statement of your vision. Your vision is a description of what your fulfilled destiny will look like. This can be described within the context of the purpose-related benefits which will accrue to you and to others and the effect upon a larger community or future generations.

Your mission statement. This is the statement of your life's purpose, your fundamental values, and the work you intend to do in accordance with the fulfillment of that purpose. Your personal mission statement is similar in construction to mission statements written on an organizational level, such as the *American Red Cross* example quoted earlier.

A description of the strategies and tactics that will serve the mission. This includes a description of the strategic ways in which you will apply and leverage your assets in order to achieve your goals. These assets include:

1. Your gifts, talents, and other attributes.

2. Your financial, human, and other resources including your life properties (life space, life volume, life texture, and life light).

3. Your strengths (understood in contrast to your weaknesses).

Based on the strategies you develop, you can develop tactical approaches that will support your strategic endeavors. (For example: Assume that your strategy is to make financial planning available to blue collar workers who expect to receive pensions upon retirement. One of your tactics might be to hold seminars at large companies for those employees who plan to retire within the next five years.)

A list and description of goals to be achieved. Goals divide your journey into manageable, productive segments that can be easily evaluated for their effectiveness. Arrange your goals into groupings according to timeframes. Feel free to adjust the suggested categories shown in the figure below to better suit your purpose.

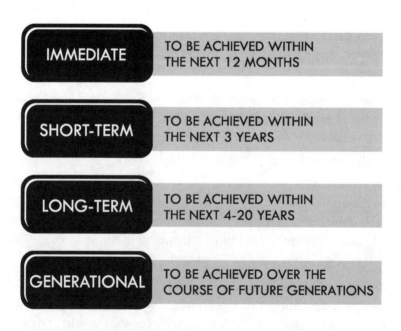

IMMEDIATE — TO BE ACHIEVED WITHIN THE NEXT 12 MONTHS

SHORT-TERM — TO BE ACHIEVED WITHIN THE NEXT 3 YEARS

LONG-TERM — TO BE ACHIEVED WITHIN THE NEXT 4-20 YEARS

GENERATIONAL — TO BE ACHIEVED OVER THE COURSE OF FUTURE GENERATIONS

A description of available opportunities and existing threats. These are the opportunities and threats you uncovered in your feasibility study. Your strategic life plan should include your plan to exploit these opportunities and mitigate or eliminate any threats in order to support the fulfillment of your mission, the execution of your strategies and tactics, and the achievement of your goals.

An assessment of the cost and a statement of commitment to accept the reasonable burden associated with your destiny fulfillment. Describe what it will cost you to fulfill your destiny. Include the range of sacrifices you will need to make including any physical and financial demands, requirements as to location, affects upon family life, and the sacrifice of conflicting desires and lesser priorities.

Consider writing a series of strategic life plans, each of which covers the key areas of your life (spiritual, social, financial, professional, family, etc.). Doing so will help you harmonize the many facets of your life into a balanced, comprehensive design.

Engrave It Upon Your Mind

You recognize the importance of committing your strategic life plan to paper. But your strategic life plan must also be written upon your mind and heart. You'll remember that writing your strategic life plan helps you assimilate it; reading and re-reading your plan on a regular basis (daily is best!) will cause it to become part of you.

The writing of your strategic life plan is not an exercise. It is the strategic act of framing your life and destiny. The purpose of your plan is to promote the purpose of your life. Once it is written, take time to interact with your strategic life plan; revise it if necessary. Do not allow your strategic life plan to be filed away and forgotten. Don't treat it as an historic record of what once was or what might have been. Be sure that it continues to be relevant over the course of time.

The strategic life plan that is committed to paper *and* written on your mind becomes the very bricks and mortar of your watchtower—the structure that is built upon high ground (providing an unobstructed view which continually refreshes your elevated perspective) *and* a defensive structure from which you can repel attacks against your dream.

Your strategic life plan bolsters your awareness of the big picture and reinforces your understanding of your place and your role in this world. It is an informative and strategic document designed to guide the building—and the living—of your strategic life.

Write your strategic life plan on paper and then write it on your mind. Stick with the plan and watch your strategic life happen!

PART III

WATCH YOUR STRATEGIC LIFE HAPPEN

9

Unleash the Power of Your Goals

*The person who makes a success of living is the one who sees his goal
and aims for it unswervingly.* [1] —Cecil B. DeMille

You have entered the final countdown to the launch of your strategic life and living your dream. You are suited up in intentionality, driven by passion and desire. Your strategic life plan has been documented. It is both written and engraved upon your mind. You are poised at the brink of lift-off and the engines of your dream are beginning to rumble. But how will you generate the necessary thrust to get your strategic life off the ground?

Simple. By unleashing the power of your goals. Harnessed within these dream-launching fuel cells is the energy of enthusiasm and the force of motivation to propel you into your destiny. Your strategic life plan has already organized the elements of this chain reaction and you have run down your prelaunch checklist:

> *Your mission has been declared.*
>
> *Your vision is in place.*
>
> *You have stated your goals.*
>
> *Your strategies and tactics are defined.*
>
> *Opportunities have been sighted.*

Threats have been exposed.

The price of your dream has been settled.

Combustion is imminent. You are ready to enter a fully intentional, proactive way of being and doing. With the thrust provided by your goals, you are prepared to lead your well-planned mission, goal . . . by goal . . . by goal.

Your careful strategic planning has positioned you for *increased effectiveness* in every destiny-inspired endeavor. No longer will you cross your fingers and hope for something good to happen. Instead, you will run with your vision and watch expectantly as your destiny unfurls.

This is the benefit of ownership. You have taken ownership of your destiny to become the CEO of an expanding enterprise—your strategic life. Instead of jumping through hoops labeled *One size fits all,* you are making purposeful, one-of-a-kind strides toward your desired outcomes. You *know* who you are and what you were created to accomplish—and you are thoroughly prepared to live it.

Your strategic life plan has infused your life pursuits with *transformative power.* The waters have been stirred; everything stagnant or unproductive is infused with new vitality. Listless efforts, lost hopes, and fading passions are reanimated. You are being transformed from within and positioned to become an agent of change in the lives of others.

Your strategic life plan is also *timely.* The rollout of your destiny is neither overdue nor premature. Instead, your goals, strategies, tactics, opportunities (and even the threats lurking in your life space) are wired to your destiny timetable and will transpire in a timely manner.

Your strategic life is not tentative or random. The days of wandering and wondering are *over.*

Goal-Powered Progress

Your goals are connected to your destiny code and therefore to your strategic life plan. Well-defined goals (and well-formed outcomes) impart new energy into your circumstances. They transform the formless, vacant areas of life into fruitful enterprises by providing structure, purpose, and order.

Structure. Goal-oriented people are time and energy conscious; they avoid aimless pursuits and they allow their goals to bring form and direction to their efforts. By adhering to goals, their lives take on the structure needed to accommodate the unfolding of their dreams.

Goals shape your efforts and therefore your outcomes. They prevent you from being vague or noncommittal. Because they promote proactivity, goals help clarify priorities so you can stick with your strategies and keep your desired outcomes on track.

Purpose. When your goals are in harmony with your life's calling, you are free to live out your intentions. Instead of wondering where the cards will fall, you wake up each day with a picture of your destination in mind and you proceed purposefully in the direction of that destination. That sense of purpose will govern your time expenditures and help you avoid ruts and rabbit trails.

Order. When you embrace a healthy measure of structure and are guided by purpose, you eliminate confusion and the indecision it propagates. You become persistently decisive and more likely to experience the systematic development of your destiny. Your well-directed choices will promote an atmosphere of order, an environment in which life's many pieces are easily fitted in place to form the big picture of your dream.

Your destiny-driven goals will always point you in the right direction. Even when skies are dark or the seasons shift unexpectedly, your goals will lead you and help you to maintain your grip on your dream. With this kind of enduring clarity, you will continue to build upon the strong foundation you poured in the beginning and you will avoid the disappointment and complaints that result from not having what you want.

Interact With Your Goals

Your goals do not exist in a vacuum; they are achieved through your continued interaction with them. This interaction involves discerning the quality of your activity, determining the nature of your goals, and monitoring the progress of your goals.

Discern the quality of your activity. To ensure steady progress and minimize misfires, you'll want to discern the quality of your activity in pursuit of your goals. Become familiar with and able to identify three key categories of activity:

ESSENTIAL ACTIVITIES—Essential activities are those which are necessary to the achievement of your goals. These activities lead to destiny fulfillment by enhancing your effectiveness, promoting steady progress, and supporting your purpose.

Essential activities are most effective when they are performed according to the order your goals suggest. The familiar analogy of the cart and the horse applies. Both the cart and the horse are essential; you can't accomplish your task if one or the other is missing. However, unless the horse is placed before the cart, the well-intended essentials will not produce the desired outcome.

Another word about essential activities—they remain essential whether or not you enjoy doing them. You've heard the expression *successful people do what others are unwilling to do*. Too often we succumb to the misguided belief that those who achieve their destinies have a special ability to enjoy the tasks despised by the rest of us. The truth is that successful people are intentional and have therefore disciplined themselves to do the essentials, whether or not they enjoy doing them. This sacrifice is part of the fair price they have agreed to pay to realize their dreams.

 BASED ON THE GOALS STATED IN YOUR STRATEGIC LIFE PLAN, MAKE A LIST OF SEVEN ACTIVITIES THAT ARE ESSENTIAL TO ACHIEVING YOUR DREAM. DESCRIBE HOW OMITTING THESE ACTIVITIES WOULD IMPACT YOUR DESTINY ACHIEVEMENT.

FULFILLING ACTIVITIES—These are the activities that move you closer to your desired outcomes while producing feelings of well-being and the sense that you are living the "good life." Among these activities are those that cause you to feel fully alive and completely in your element.

Prioritize these activities with care so that you can invest sufficient time in their pursuit. They are tied to your destiny code and will advance your mission. They also revitalize your emotions by providing an outlet through which to express your passions. The investment of your time and energy in these fulfilling activities will strengthen you from within and improve your attitude, performance, and results while causing the journey to be aesthetically pleasing to you.

 Describe one or more goal-related activities that bring you the greatest fulfillment. Explain how these activities help to recharge your physical and emotional battery.

Unfulfilling activities—These are the activities you'll want to identify and avoid. They may be rote functions that have become habitual through inside-the-box thinking. They drain energy, waste time, and bring discouragement. Therefore they hinder healthy interaction with your goals.

Unfulfilling activities must be distinguished from the essential activities you would prefer not to do, but that promote goal achievement. Unfulfilling activities produce results on the negative side of the ledger and are often punishing in their overall effect on you.

 Identify three unfulfilling activities in which you regularly engage. Consider and note the factors that have motivated you to continue in these activities until now.

Determine the nature of your goals. Always be selective about your activities and recognize that not all goals lead to well-being. Take care not to rationalize the setting of goals that may be driven by wrong motives. It is essential that your goals be vetted. Be transparent; identify any pursuits that are driven by emotional neediness or other forms of unfinished business. Stick to goals that lead to well-being and result in long-term benefit for all involved parties.

Consider the following three categories of goals that lead to well-being:

GOALS THAT PROMOTE INTIMACY—This involves intimacy in the broad sense. It is the desire to engage in close, reciprocal relationships. Relationships of this kind are productive and authentic, not one-sided or shallow. These relationships run deep and will cost you something. They are based in honesty, integrity, and compassion, and they produce interaction that fosters emotional health and personal growth for both parties. Goals that promote intimacy give full expression to our humanity and enrich our life experiences, not at the expense of others, but for the benefit of all.

GOALS THAT ENGAGE OUR SPIRITUALITY—Whether or not you can re-member the Peggy Lee song, "Is That All There Is?" the question posed by the diva is a universal one. We know instinctively that life is more than an accident of nature. We long to find the larger context in which life's fullest meaning is revealed. We desire to transcend *self* and be part of some-thing larger than life; therefore, we benefit from setting goals that address this need. Goals that engage spirituality help us keep our motives in check by providing a worldview that extends beyond concerns for self.

GOALS THAT CONSIDER GENERATIVITY—In Chapter 8, we talked about generativity in terms of the legacy we leave. You'll remember that genera-tivity is the commitment to concerns outside your four walls and even be-yond your generation. Generativity causes us to recognize the impact we can have beyond our lifetimes. Goals that address generativity enable us to plan for this impact to be part of the achievement of our dreams.

Monitor the progress of your goals. Finally, interact with your goals by monitoring your progress and making any necessary adjustments. Sound goals provide benchmarks which delineate your advancement toward dream achievement and increased well-being.

Allow your goals to provide this important feedback so that you can as-sess your overall development. Examine these benchmarks carefully. Ask yourself whether your progress is adequate. Determine whether the achievement of your goals is increasing your sense of well-being. If not, find out why not. Could it be that your goals are misguided? Or, is an un-sound belief system causing you to discredit your progress and subcon-sciously undermine your momentum?

If disappointment results from the monitoring of your benchmarks, it could be that you are limiting the scope of your achievements through fear-based behaviors or small, inside-the-box thinking. Disappointment could also be alerting you to goals that overlook your need for intimacy, spirituality, and generativity.

Keep in mind that when you are determined to close the gaps between intended outcomes and the results you actually experience, it is best to uncover these deficiencies sooner rather than later. Disappointing results needn't be devastating. You are fully empowered to make effective adjustments in response to shortcomings.

Strategic living does not mean having a plan that is set in stone; it means being willing to own your outcomes and remain flexible enough to make the most of every opportunity to improve.

Benchmark

A standard by which something can be measured or judged.[2]

Elevate Your Enthusiasm

The American Heritage Dictionary defines *enthusiasm* in part as "great excitement for or interest in a subject or cause."[3] In strategic life planning, the cause that generates excitement is your *vision* and the goals which are based in that vision. When vision and goals are based upon purpose, "great excitement" is the result. This elevated enthusiasm will affect your overall perspective and, therefore, your behavior.

Our focus is on the big picture of your life and the effects of enthusiasm on the achievement of your dream. But enthusiasm works at every level—and at every age. Whether you are a senior citizen or still in your teens, you would probably agree that young people often have to be coaxed out of bed on school days. That is, until something sparks enthusiasm for a classmate of the opposite sex. Suddenly the inspired teen can't wait to get to school. He or she has a daily goal—to interact with that special someone.

That is the power of enthusiasm—it accentuates the upside of every situation. We have more fun doing whatever it is that we do. Obstacles and inconveniences are minimized and life's benefits become more apparent.

Enthusiasm reminds us that we can do anything we set our minds on doing. It greases the wheels of progress and sustains momentum. It is not the result of a caffeine jolt—genuine enthusiasm comes from within. It is an elevated perspective that is linked to your purpose; it will cause you to be excited and eager about the work ahead.

Enthusiasm is a destiny-linked mood elevator; it lifts your spirits, increases energy, and enlivens the pursuit of your goals. It lifts you outside the box and drowns out the negativity of others. It makes you buoyant and unsinkable. You'll be like the biplane mentioned (albeit, facetiously) by the Wright Brothers that "stays up because it doesn't have the time to fall."[4]

Those who live strategically see each moment as another opportunity. They are as enthusiastic about work as they are about play. They often find it hard to distinguish between the two!

Fuel Your Motivation

Ralph Waldo Emerson said, "Nothing great was ever achieved without enthusiasm."[5] The reason—enthusiasm is generated by purpose and it, in turn, generates motivation. The dynamics of motivation are powerful and critical to destiny fulfillment.

Sustained motivation is not externally induced. It is what I call an "inside job," meaning that if it is genuine, it will come from within. Here's how it develops: When you have a goal in mind that you see as being worthwhile, you become enthusiastic about pursuing that goal. This enthusiasm motivates you; it engages your core criteria, including your passion, in order to accomplish the goal. You become more clearly and strongly intentional. When your motivation is fueled in this way, you can take your vision and run with it—and you will be able to run with it all the way to the fulfillment of your dream!

When enthusiasm sparks this internal, premium-grade motivation, the chain reaction foretold in your strategic life plan is ignited.

The higher the level of motivation, the higher the level of commitment. When you are motivated, it is easier to make a commitment to your cause. Because you are enthusiastic and motivated, you see the price of your dream as small in comparison to the value of your desired outcomes. Therefore you gladly make the necessary sacrifices.

When you operate in this way, your commitment level continually cycles higher. Because you have invested in your dream, you are less likely to walk away from it. And as you move ever closer to your desired outcomes, you are prone to invest even more, thereby becoming more committed every step of the way.

The higher the level of commitment, the higher the level of achievement. The more committed you are the more you will invest, therefore the higher your rate of gain. Think of it in terms of a bank account—the more you put in, the more you can take out. With an internally generated level of motivation set in motion by enthusiasm for a worthy cause (your destiny), you will always have a head of steam pushing you forward. Therefore, you will attain to ever higher levels of accomplishment, fulfillment, and a greater and more fulfilling enjoyment of life's pleasures.

A word about the formation of goals that produce enthusiasm and, therefore, motivation: positive, pleasure-producing goals (consider *pleasure* here in the larger context that includes contentment, joy, and fulfillment) motivate us more powerfully than do negative, fear-based goals. Consider the distinction between these two types of motivators as shown through the following examples:

POSITIVE GOAL

TO MAINTAIN A SOUND SOCIAL AND PROFESSIONAL BALANCE SO AS TO PROVIDE A LIFESTYLE THAT MEETS MY FAMILY'S BASIC NEEDS; PROVIDES EACH FAMILY MEMBER OPPORTUNITIES FOR SOUND EMOTIONAL, SPIRITUAL, AND PHYSICAL DEVELOPMENT; ALLOWS FOR HEALTHFUL AND RESTORATIVE RECREATION; AND PROMOTES THE FULFILLMENT OF EACH MEMBER'S UNIQUE DESTINY THROUGH LOVE AND ACCEPTANCE, EDUCATION, MENTORSHIP AND A SENSE OF SECURITY.

FEAR-BASED GOAL

TO DO WHATEVER IT TAKES TO AVOID THE ANGUISH OF POVERTY AND THE DEGRADATION IT ENGENDERS; TO AVOID THE PITFALLS OF LACK INCLUDING THE DEBILITATING EXPERIENCE OF LIMITED OPPORTUNITY EXPERIENCED BY MY PARENTS. TO ENSURE THAT MY FAMILY WILL NEVER BE NEEDY OR DEPENDENT UPON ANYONE FOR ANYTHING.

Negative goals are built upon fear and upon the often unarticulated sense that undesirable outcomes are to be accepted as the norm. They cause us to fight against the dark tide, not to overcome it, but in the hopes that we will somehow manage to keep our heads above water. Negative goals cannot motivate as powerfully as positive ones because on the sub-conscious level, fear-based goals set expectations below the level of the dream.

Positive goals lift us above the failures of the past and urge us to reach for the stars. They place us outside the box where all things are possible, and they reveal the inward sense that we are worthy of experiencing good outcomes. Positive goal-setting also harmonizes with the aesthetic approach to strategic life planning and facilitates a life design you can truly enjoy.

Fine-tune Your Focus

When your strategic life plan is written upon your mind, your dreams and goals will determine the content of your consciousness. Your focus—including your thoughts and emotional states—will be affected by your goals and will naturally revolve around your intended outcomes. Your focus is critical because where you are looking is where you will go. You can fine-tune this critical focus by assessing two key aspects of every goal:

1. The nature of the goal.
2. The status of its pursuit.

The nature of your goal involves more than whether it is professional or personal, financial or artistic. The nature of your goal also involves:

The effects of your goal upon your overall life. This includes the pleasure your goal provides and the sacrifices it demands of you.

The level of the goal's priority. The priority you assign to your goal should govern the intensity of your dedication to it.

The goal's interconnectedness with other goals. This relatedness of each goal to all the others includes the way in which one goal facilitates, and is facilitated by, other goals.

The status of a goal's pursuit is revealed by the reading of benchmarks. Each goal provides a benchmark of progress toward the achievement of your dream, but each goal also has internal benchmarks of its own. These indicators provide a progress report as each step of the goal is underway. They help you measure your incremental success toward goal completion and provide insight as to any adjustments that may be necessary.

This focus, in conjunction with clear, strong intent, will help you understand where you are, where you are going, and how far you have come. The ability to pinpoint your location in relation to your destiny is critical. Without it, you will repeat the mistakes of the past. You will also overlook the finer points of your progress. This misread engenders the sense that your efforts are futile; therefore it can cause your motivation to wither, even to the point that quitting will appear to be your only option.

Here are three quick pointers on maintaining your focus:

Focus on what you have rather than what you don't have. Rather than bemoaning your weaknesses, keep your strengths in view. When you focus on what you *can* do, you'll find a way to do it. Your *doing* will affect your *being* and will also ensure further progress.

Focus on end results rather than current challenges. Maintain your elevated perspective. From up in your watchtower, you will see your challenges in the context of your opportunities and you will be able to see beyond both to the horizon of your dreams. When you are encouraged by the big picture, you will tackle the challenges and find that they aren't as intimidating as they once seemed to be. From this elevated viewpoint, dread and worry are seen for what they are: a waste of precious time and energy.

Focus on what you want rather than what you don't want. Once your goals are established, walk away from what isn't working for you. Keep your sights set on your stated goals so that your thoughts, behaviors, and actions will remain aligned with your intentions. This will keep you moving consciously and subconsciously toward the life you have designed.

> Nothing can stop the man with the right mental attitude from achieving his goal; nothing on earth can help the man with the wrong mental attitude.[6] —Thomas Jefferson

Protect Your Priorities

With your goals dictating the content of your consciousness, your priorities will fall into place organically. You'll recall the analogy of the general in the field: Once his strategic plan is established, it is easy to form tactical decisions. The same is true of your strategic life plan; once your plan is in place and your goals are established in accordance with that plan, your priorities become apparent. To capitalize on this clear sense of priority, you have to stick with your plan.

This seems like a statement of the obvious, yet it bears repeating. Too often we drop the plan due to distractions, discouragement, or disappointment. Yet it is when you face these temporary setbacks that your plan becomes most helpful. Your strategic life plan and the clear goals it generates will help you cling to the path of destiny when all hell breaks loose in your life.

To protect your priorities, simply work your plan and plan your work. Keep your goals in clear view. Avoid developing affection for pursuits that are outside of your plan. The seemingly harmless rabbit trail can cost you more time and energy than you might realize. Even a slight drift from your strategic path can send you significantly off course—and quickly.

Your best defense against misplaced priorities is to begin with a disciplined approach. Decide beforehand how you will respond to diversions. When tempted to get offtrack, take a moment to refocus by asking yourself how the suggested activity fits in with your goals. If you discover that a pursuit is not aligned with your goals, simply say, "No. This is not on my schedule because it is not a priority."

If you find that you frequently veer off course, check inside for any unfinished business. Search out any misbeliefs that remain irreconcilable to the lifestyle and outcomes you desire. Never make peace with self-sabotaging thoughts. Defy and uproot them. Get on with the business of living instead of *reliving* the outcomes that you don't want.

Protect your priorities and your destiny by always bearing in mind that your dream has a price. Your strategic life plan declares your commitment to that price and to the worthy outcomes your sacrifice will yield. Dig your heels in and stick to the plan. Don't sample alternatives or forfeit your best life plan by settling for something less. Assign a high priority to the tasks connected with worthy goals and be determined to follow through. It sounds simple, but it is not always easy to do. If it were, everyone would achieve greatness.

Money Is a Consequence

When discussing priorities, the question of money always comes up. Where does money fit into your goals? To answer this question let's first return to the subject of enthusiasm. Genuine enthusiasm is generated by the purpose for which you were created. Enthusiasm in turn releases the motivation you need to accomplish your purpose.

Money is not a purpose; money is a consequence of the pursuit of purpose. When you commit to your life's mission and remain faithful to it, the resources you need—both financial and otherwise—will come. Until you experience this steady stream of resources (and forever afterward) *stick to the plan.* Money will test your commitment to the vision. If you're not prepared for the test, money will supplant your purpose, undermine your values, and leave you feeling accomplished, but empty.

That said, prosperity is not a curse but a blessing. However, an untoward preoccupation with money (what the Bible calls "the *love* of money,"[7]) is not a blessing at all. It reveals the presence of unfinished business with which you will need to deal—decisively. The love of money can draw a tantalizing picture of a life that looks good, smells good, and tastes good, but amounts to something far less than your destiny offers.

Saddle Up and Ride!

You're ready to take the goal-powered ride of your life. Don't wait for lightning to strike. Instead, take what you have and what you know and light up the atmosphere with the enthusiasm your dream ignites. Stay plugged into your destiny code. Mine its depths. Seize upon the capabilities, competencies, and resources embedded within—and ride.

Don't keep your enthusiasm to yourself. Become a carrier of expectancy and hope for the future. Infect everyone you know and watch the tide rise around you. Then when excitement is exploding in your heart and success is erupting in your circumstances, remain humble, realizing that all of the goodness you have to share is for a purpose that is bigger than life itself.

You are a miracle waiting to happen.

10

FACE DOWN FEAR

Fear and anxiety are debilitating emotions. They are interest paid in advance on a debt you may never owe.[1] —John Maxwell

Why talk about fear now? The answer is simple: Unbounded fear is the enemy of destiny. It is a cruel and illegitimate taskmaster known to exact a high price from those whom it enslaves.

Still, the human response of fear is a fact of life with which even the bravest warriors would concur. One of them, General Ferdinand Foch of France, spoke plainly about the universality of fear saying, "None but a coward dares to boast that he has never known fear."[2]

Everyone is acquainted with fear. The butterflies, racing heartbeat, quivering voice, loss of appetite—have been experienced by all of us. These sensations are never pleasant; yet fear is not always bad. Some fears are well-placed and aid in our self-preservation. If we had not been taught a healthy fear of the power of electricity, we might be tempted to soak in the tub with a plugged-in radio perched nearby. Instead, because we are aware of the negative consequences, we protect against being electrocuted.

A healthy respect for hazard helps us to draw reasonable boundaries and make informed decisions. It is only when fear overruns reason that we find ourselves enslaved by it. If you fear being electrocuted in the tub while the overhead light is turned on, then your fear is misplaced. Instead of forming reasonable boundaries and making informed decisions, you will retreat from beneficial activities and live under the shadow of a nonexistent threat.

Misplaced or compulsive fears are dream-killers. When we entertain them, we withdraw within ourselves and succumb to distorted perceptions. In this state of constant alarm, rational thinking is distorted. We become immersed in confusion and are dragged under by currents of uncertainty. Left unchecked, errant fears drain vitality and deplete the emotional and physical resources needed for strategic living.

There is only one way to be free from dream-killing fear and that is to first expose it and then face it head on.

Understand the Fear Factor

For our purposes, we will assume that fears fall into two broad categories, namely, *well-placed* and *misplaced* fears. However, as we address the subject of fear, we will focus solely on the negative variety—*misplaced* fear. The first step is to understand where this fear begins and how it operates.

We have established that fear is a fact of life. It is an emotional and physical response to any stimulus perceived to be threatening. In other words, fear is a symptom produced by something that is happening now or has happened in the past.

Events and experiences that cause fear become part of human memory. Therefore they help form our internal belief structures. Through the replaying of these memories, fear can become an entrenched response so that we find ourselves reacting to present and future experiences purely on the basis of something that has happened in the past. This ingrained fear will surface over and over again, even when the original experience is completely unrelated to new circumstances.

Take the example of a little girl who has been abandoned by her father. The trauma to the deserted child is profound and produces in the youngster powerful emotional responses. These responses are triggered by the uncertainty the child is facing *and* by internal, often unspoken, assumptions the child makes in an effort to explain the parent's actions.

The following assumptions are commonly included in the rationale of a child dealing with abandonment:

Dad left me because I did something bad.

Because I am bad, Dad doesn't love me anymore.

If Dad doesn't love me anymore, then I am unworthy to be loved.

Therefore, I deserve to be rejected by others…

And I expect to suffer the pain of rejection in future significant relationships.

Admittedly, there is typically much more to this kind of scenario than we can cover here; therefore, this example is over-simplified. Yet it is a common story and serves as a valid illustration of how chronic fears develop.

Without a great deal of attention to this wounded child's emotional and psychological needs, her fear of abandonment will remain part of her unfinished business. Her pain will not be resolved simply by the passage of time. Instead, the pain experienced in the original event will likely become attached to the girl's memory where it will be relived on a conscious and subconscious level for years to come.

Let's follow our fictitious girl into the future to see how the fear of abandonment continues to operate in her life. Years later, she is a young married woman whose mate is a loving and devoted husband. They share a stable, validating, and non-threatening relationship. The husband is faithful and attentive; yet, instead of feeling affirmed, the young wife grows increasingly insecure and distrustful. Though her husband professes and demonstrates his love for her, she feels threatened by every woman with whom he comes into contact. Because of her underlying fear, the young wife sees these inconsequential relationships as direct threats to her security.

The wife's increasing distrust is a form of misplaced fear. It is not a reaction to the character of her relationship with her husband. Nor is it about the women she finds so threatening. Instead, it is rooted in the *expectation of abandonment* which she carries within. This expectation is supported not only by the memory of her desertion as a child, but by the sense of shame the awful event engendered.

Remember that the little girl assumed responsibility for her dad's departure. She believed that she did something bad; more importantly, she believed that because she did something bad, she *is* bad. That is the essence of shame; it is the sense that there is something intrinsically wrong with one's *self*. Shame overwhelms self-image and, once accepted, becomes the bedrock of one's identity.

Until shame is uprooted, it continues to speak—and *loudly*. The voice of shame is fear. The young woman lives in constant fear of being abandoned by her husband because she believes abandonment is what she deserves. Her interaction with her husband is therefore governed by her expectation, perpetuating her fear and causing her to respond in inappropriate ways. Unless she deals with the root of her fear, the woman will unwittingly drive a wedge in her marital relationship. Then if the marriage fails, her misbeliefs will be reinforced and her fear will escalate, perpetuating a cycle of poor outcomes.

It is easy to see how the dream—in this case, the dream of a happy, fruitful marriage—can be undermined by the enemy called *fear*.

Know the Enemy of Your Dream

To face down fear strategically, you'll want to first know and understand its character. Never underestimate the impact of fear; it is a deceiving and disorienting force. Unless it is checked, it *will* steal your dream and undermine your best efforts.

Let's examine the ways in which fear infiltrates some of the workings of destiny we have already discussed. This understanding will facilitate the ability to recognize fear, resist its advances, and root it out.

Fear keeps you from developing and maintaining an elevated perspective. Regardless of the form it takes, unbounded fear always promotes oppression, the sense of being weighed down and unable to cope with everyday life. Focus becomes inward and vision grows increasingly myopic.

Instead of being perched in the watchtower where the big picture of your dream is visible, attention becomes restricted to life's immediate foreground. This narrow territory includes your current emotional state (which has been commandeered by fear) and the obstacles directly in front of you. From this low vantage point, upcoming opportunities are less visible and less likely to be acted upon. Forward motion is stymied and fear is reinforced by the hopelessness that develops in the absence of progress.

Fear restricts you to inside-the-box thinking. Whether on a subliminal or conscious level, fear causes us to expect the worst. Therefore, fear magnifies the human aversion to risk and overshadows our expectations of reward. This self-limiting dynamic is also self-perpetuating. The more we avoid stepping outside the box, the less access we have to opportunity and the more steeped in the status quo we become. Without the confidence-building that is gained through accomplishment, we become increasingly fearful of stepping outside the box.

Fear chains you to unfinished business and denies you the clarity to move forward. When we are fear-driven, we are more susceptible to burrs, including unforgiveness, victim mentality, pessimism, procrastination, passivity, and timidity. Fear also prompts us to protect our blind spots including any self-sabotaging misbeliefs that keep us preoccupied with the past. This fixation on unfinished business clouds our vision and covers the path to destiny with emotional clutter.

Fear causes you to mislabel your seasons. Every season of life is linked to your destiny code and plays a part in the achievement of your dream. But not every season looks positive on the surface. Discerning the purpose of each season requires clarity; but when we are fearful, confusion reigns and truth is masked. Therefore the seasons designed to unpack the missing pieces of our destiny puzzle can be mistakenly identified as nothing more than periods of loss or defeat.

Fear fixes your outcomes in the negative. Because fear lowers perspective, diminishes expectations, fosters adherence to old paradigms, causes us to cling to the past, and confuses the seasons of life, the desired outcomes we so carefully define are inadvertently capped. The resulting disappointment then reinforces the fears that caused us to retreat in the first place.

Now that you understand the key ways in which fear chips away at your dream, here is bigger and better news for you to digest: *You are fully equipped to neutralize fear with a rational approach.* When you remain rational in the face of fear, it becomes virtually transparent and, without fear's ability to confuse, it has no power! There is no fear, no matter how deeply entrenched it may be, that cannot be defused. So let's explore—and render transparent!—some common fears encountered by those who live strategically.

The Fear of Rejection

Our abandonment illustration also reveals the way that rejection strikes at one's sense of self. While rejection itself is painful, it is the *fear of rejection* that produces ongoing harm.

Because the young woman in our story accepted a shame-based identity, she lived in fear of future rejection. And because she believed that her authentic identity was what caused her to be rejected in the first place, she forfeited the freedom to be her best self—her *authentic* self.

The same is true of our individual destinies. When the fear of rejection drives our behavior, we are tricked into believing that being "real" is dangerous. Therefore we conceal authentic identity and contrive new versions of ourselves. In an effort to avoid being hurt, we wear the masks that we believe will ensure affirmation. We mistakenly invest ourselves in the hope that a false identity will be more acceptable to others (and to ourselves) than the real person underneath it.

Unfortunately, masks are heavier than they look. In order to "sell" an inauthentic identity, the mask-wearer has to *perform,* or act out, the assumed identity. This performance mentality is adopted in the hopes of diverting the focus of others onto *what we do* instead of *who we are.* So, instead of *being,* we work hard at *doing* things to gain the affirmation we crave.

The price of the masquerade is manifold. First, we sacrifice the authentic identity that is integrally connected with our destiny code. As a result, we become self-conscious and tentative in our interaction and unwilling to state our desires honestly. We morph ourselves into the characters we think others prefer. In essence, we try to live out their dream and we sacrifice our own.

If you give in to the demands of the mask, you will find it impossible to appreciate or benefit from your individuality. You will avoid putting your attributes on the table for fear they will not be good enough. Therefore others will be unable to see and appreciate the greatness within you. In an attempt to protect yourself from rejection, you will have unintentionally denied your destiny code and the unique factor linked to it.

The fear of rejection is potent, but it is not omnipotent. You already have an entire toolkit with which to overcome this fear. One of your tools is to reacquaint yourself with the contents of your strategic life inventory and renew the vision of how formidable you really are.

The other is to climb back into your watchtower and reabsorb the big picture of your dream. Allow your strategic life plan to remind you of all you stand to gain by being authentic and present to the moment. Re-engage the full sensory experience of your dream and recapture the balanced perspective of your future. With the force of your dream backing you up, you are empowered to reject the fear of rejection.

Fatalism

The acceptance of all things and events as inevitable; submission to fate[3]

The Fear of Failure

Because of the way humans are wired, we don't like to fail. Yet, like fear, failure is a fact of life. The clash between these opposing realities creates undeniable emotional tension. Add in the weight of any unfinished business (including poor self-image and the stinging memories of past failures) and you have a recipe for another dream-killer: *the fear of failure.*

In an effort to circumvent this fear, we often pave complex, costly routes around it. These failure-avoidance methods are plentiful. Let's explore a few.

Fatalism. One way to avoid failure is to prove in advance that we cannot control outcomes related to the dream. We can do this by donning a protective layer of fatalism which says, *Whatever will be, will be. Whether I succeed or fail is not up to me.* If we believe outcomes are rigged, we tend to approach the dream half-heartedly and we avoid accountability for disappointing outcomes. The price for this form of failure-avoidance is high; fatalism protects against failure by removing the possibility of success.

Fatalism leads to imprisonment in the comfort zone. From this potential-less location, life space is under-utilized and opportunities wither on the vine; weaknesses are easily concealed and the tendency to over-rely on strengths is exaggerated, creating self-sabotaging blind spots. As the name implies, fatalism produces death of the dream.

Task avoidance. Until we face down the fear of failure, we skip doing the not-so-fun things successful people are willing to do. The possibility of failure serves as a built-in excuse to avoid tasks that don't provide immediate gratification. In this way, we resign ourselves to the mediocre and we short-circuit the achievement of our dreams.

Lack of experimentation. When the fear of failure overwhelms the desire to succeed, experimentation seems extravagant and even futile. Imagination shrivels and creativity is cast aside. Our best efforts are put on hold; we set them aside for a day that will never come—the day we can perform in absolute safety and with complete assurance that our outcomes will reflect on us favorably.

Lack of interaction with goals and priorities. The enslavement to fear paralyzes us. It keeps our dreams, goals, and visions trapped on the pages of a well-intended strategic life plan. Instead of interacting with our goals, we allow the fear of under-performing to keep us from destiny's stage. Because we're focused on self-protection, we subconsciously replace forward-looking, dream-driven goals with backward efforts designed to keep us safe.

Lack of outcome assessment. The fear of failure predisposes us to avoid honest assessment of our outcomes. Because past outcome gaps have caused us memorable and ongoing pain, we would just as soon not discover any new shortfalls. Therefore we fail to make helpful adjustments and we disallow the creation of fitting solutions. Ironically, by ignoring our outcomes, we ensure the very outcome gaps of which we are fearful and we lock ourselves into a lifestyle of failure.

The best antidote to the fear of failure is an appreciation of the fact that imperfect outcomes create perfect opportunities for future success.

Give yourself permission to make mistakes (we are all going to make mistakes anyway!). Remind yourself that success is achieved incrementally. It is not based upon a single performance. Success is based on persistence and percentages.

You don't have to bat .1000 to succeed; you just have to stay in the game.

The Fear of the Cost

Every dream has a price, and sometimes that price causes sticker shock. While it is good to have a big picture view of your dream, it is also important to remember that the price of your dream is never paid in a single lump sum. Instead, the cost is paid the same way rewards are received— over time. We plunk down the price of the destiny ticket little by little and by the time each installment comes due, we have gained more strength and are better able to make the payment.

Yet the cost remains, and the fear of paying it must be reckoned with. Some people find a way to keep the cost in perspective. Others fret over it. Still others decide against paying up.

Joseph Jaworski's words quoted earlier bear repeating:

> Most of us tend to avoid taking the journey to discover and serve our purpose. We refuse the call because deep down we know that to cooperate with fate brings not only great personal power, but great personal responsibility as well.[4]

Anything worth having will cost you. To ignore the fair price of a worthy dream would be foolish. But to consider the price outside the larger context of the commensurate reward would be just as silly.

Those who are determined to live strategically find a reason to pay the price without grumbling. That is not to say that their decisions in favor of the dream are made casually. Quite the contrary: Those who live strategically know what they are getting themselves into, at least as much as it can be known. They decide to move forward willingly because they believe the rewards are worthy of the sacrifice.

Dreams come in all shapes and sizes, but the dynamics are the same. Imagine for a moment the consideration that must be given to the decision to run for president of the United States. Of all the positions in the world, this one offers perhaps the greatest historical recognition and the most power. However, the sacrifices required to run for president and to become the leader of the free world are massive.

For as much as two years, the presidential candidate must endure the rigors of campaigning. If that run is successful, he or she will face four to eight years in what is, arguably, the most demanding job on earth. The challenges of running and then serving as president are too numerous to mention. Let's sample four of them:

> *Eighteen-hour days on the campaign trail.*
>
> *Long campaign jaunts away from home and family.*
>
> *Financial sacrifices including the sale of assets and suspension of business associations that represent a conflict of interest.*
>
> *The immense emotional and physical pressures of leading a nation.*

There is plenty of downside to the presidential dream; yet for those who are called, the drawbacks are recognized as being just one side of a two-sided coin. For the presidential dream to be lived, the candidate has to face down the fear and have a sincere appreciation of *why* the dream is worth the cost.

One caveat before we continue: Not everyone who decides against a presidential run bows out due to fear. There are perfectly good, *un-fearful* reasons not to enter this highly-charged arena. For one, it is not in everybody's destiny code to run for or serve as president. The cost/reward equation will never add up for those who pursue a dream that is not genuinely theirs. But if you have an authentic vision—for the presidency or any other dream—paying the price is the only satisfactory choice.

The following figure uses the example of the presidential bid to illustrate the way that fear can cause you to rationalize your way out of your dream.

THE COST OF THE DREAM	COST ASSESSMENT
EIGHTEEN-HOUR DAYS ON THE CAMPAIGN TRAIL	FEAR-BASED RATIONALE: I KNOW MY DREAM IS REAL BUT I DON'T THINK I HAVE THE STAMINA TO LIVE IT. DESTINY-BASED TRUTH: I WAS CREATED WITH THE CAPACITY TO FULFILL MY DESTINY.
LONG CAMPAIGN JAUNTS AWAY FROM HOME AND FAMILY	FEAR-BASED RATIONALE: I'M A CREATURE OF HABIT. LIFE ON THE ROAD WOULD LEAVE ME DISORIENTED AND INEFFECTIVE. DESTINY-BASED TRUTH: DESTINY IS ALWAYS OUTSIDE THE BOX. I WAS CREATED TO THRIVE THERE.
FINANCIAL SACRIFICES INCLUDING THE SALE OF ASSETS AND SUSPENSION OF BUSINESS ASSOCIATIONS THAT REPRESENT A CONFLICT OF INTEREST	FEAR-BASED RATIONALE: I'M AFRAID TO SACRIFICE WHAT I HAVE WORKED SO HARD TO GAIN. DESTINY-BASED TRUTH: THE GAINS MADE UP TO THIS POINT WERE DESIGNED TO LEAD ME HERE. THE PURSUIT OF MY FULFILLED DESTINY WILL PROVIDE THE RESOURCES I NEED TO CONTINUE.
THE IMMENSE EMOTIONAL AND PHYSICAL PRESSURES OF LEADING A NATION	FEAR-BASED RATIONALE: THERE IS NO RESPITE FROM THE DEMANDS OF THE PRESIDENCY. I'M NOT SURE I COULD HANDLE THE PRESSURE, PHYSICALLY OR EMOTIONALLY. DESTINY-BASED TRUTH: THE COST OF THE DREAM IS GREAT; BUT SO ARE THE PHYSICAL AND EMOTIONAL COSTS OF AN UNFULFILLED LIFE. MY DREAM WILL GENERATE ENTHUSIASM FOR THE WORK INVOLVED.

Make an Accurate Cost/Reward Analysis

Everyone with a dream has a choice to make: Whether to face down the fears associated with paying the price of that dream or to risk missing the dream altogether. Follow the steps below to create your personalized version of the above figure. Use this exercise to help you assess your fears of the cost.

1. Consider and describe the costs related to the fulfillment of your destiny. List those costs on your personalized chart.

2. Identify and describe any fears related to these costs. Use what you have learned about your dreams, your destiny code, and your attributes to ascertain which thoughts are fear-based rationales and list them on your chart.

3. Debunk the fear-based rationales with destiny-based truths and record them on your chart.

4. Consider writing those truths on an index card. Keep the card in your purse or pocket and read it whenever fear strikes.

Your Dream Is a Fear-Killer

Temptations to live in fear are easily found. Strategic dreamers know this and are always prepared to look their fears in the eye and face them down.

You already have the best strategy for beating fear—the dream itself. We've explored the many positive effects of the dream upon our lives. These effects are fear-killers and will help you keep your dream alive!

The dream attunes you to destiny fulfillment. Your dream stirs in you the awareness of your destiny and helps you make life choices in support of your dream. When fear threatens, you can overcome its advance with practical responses. Do you remember the example in Chapter 3 of the marathon runner whose lifestyle is conducted with clear intentionality? This runner can face down the fear of failure by staying committed to the established daily routine. By doing the things that are proven to work, the runner will sideline fear and reach the finish line.

The dream focuses perception and produces clear priorities. When fear raises its ugly head, the marathoner deals with it the same way as with any other distraction—by focusing instead on the activities and priorities that are proven to produce positive results. In this way, an undeterred focus sustains motivation, productivity, and advancement toward the goal.

The dream directs your will. The marathoner has developed the willpower to make hard choices in pursuit of the dream. Therefore, when fear sneaks in, the runner simply relies on the same self-discipline that has powered other good choices. Instead of rolling over to fear, the runner resists the onslaught, saying, "No! Fear is a choice, and I'm choosing against it. I'm going for my dream!"

The dream redirects your emotions. When fear tempts the dedicated marathon hopeful to become depressed, overwhelmed, or self-pitying, the dream becomes a powerful means of re-centering negative emotions. Instead of being "played" by fear, the runner will use the dream of winning the marathon to re-elevate perspective and raise spirits.

The dream ignites imagination and produces vision to move forward. You may have seen the acronym *F.E.A.R.* which stands for *false evidence appearing real.* Well-placed fears deal with real hazards. Misplaced fears (worry) live primarily in the imagination. The dream of winning the marathon (or any other dream) uses the imagination to make the dream tangible. When fear strikes, the runner is able to reactivate the imagination and engage a full sensory experience. Handling the dream in this way keeps fear from turning into defeat and ensures the advancement of the dream.

The dream affects cognition. The marathoner believes that records were made to be broken, and therefore believes that everything is possible. When fear comes to steal the dream, the question is not, *How can I overcome fear?* but *How can I do anything but overcome fear?*

Success, in large part, is determined by the decisions you make concerning the experiences and emotions you choose to magnify and those you choose to minimize. Your dream is powerful. Draw on that power to help you stay focused and lock fear out of your life. When you force your fear to look your dream in the eye, fear doesn't stand a chance of winning.

The Fear Habit

"Worry is fear that has unpacked its bags and signed a long-term lease. Worry never moves out of its own accord—it has to be evicted."[5] —John Ortberg

Admit Your Fear and Move on—to the Land of Opportunity

If fear is trying to overwrite your dream, don't be surprised and don't ignore it. Experiencing fear is nothing to be ashamed of. Besides, sweeping fear under the rug only creates more unfinished business and unfinished business will keep you on the defensive.

Refuse to be boxed in by fear. Take the offense and expose your fears by first admitting they exist. Then deal with them. Remind your fear about the dream you have and remind yourself of how powerful and promising that dream is.

Talk with trustworthy people who are living strategically and find out how they handle fear. You'll be amazed to find out that those you admire are likely those people who have dealt with fear and are transparent enough to talk about it.

Facing down fear is part of the price of your dream. The price is not too high for you to pay; you already know that your dream is well worth it! So bring your fears into the light of your dream and watch them begin to evaporate.

Then get ready to live your dream like never before—by tapping into opportunity with no holds barred.

TAP INTO OPPORTUNITY

Small opportunities are often the beginning of great enterprises.[1]
—Demosthenes

After taking a used car for a test drive, the prospective buyer drove the car back to the lot. As she stepped out of the automobile, the hopeful dealer greeted her with a smile saying, "Ma'am, this car is a golden opportunity."

"Yes," replied the woman. "I heard it knocking the whole time."[2]

Sometimes opportunity knocks so plainly we can't help but notice and are quick to act. At other times opportunities park themselves somewhere in our life space and idle quietly until we detect them—or until they unceremoniously sputter out and retire to life's junk heap, the place called *What Might Have Been.*

Either way, opportunity is always present and poised for discovery. To the extent that we remain aware and are prepared and willing to act, "golden" opportunities are those with the potential to be wonderfully life-changing. It's no surprise that we are captivated by colorful tales of opportunity's blessed knock. Whether it is the story of the unsuspecting Lana Turner who was discovered while sipping a cola or the spectacular rise of new faces on televised amateur competitions, we are enthralled with legends about the moment of the "big break."

What should thrill us even more are the golden opportunities we encounter firsthand, the sterling moments in which circumstances are aligned for synergistic effect in our own lives. We pray for these moments of windfall when once-closed doors become entryways to the lives we desire to live. Afterward these moments become milestones remembered with awe, moments that forever mark the *before* and *after* epochs of our lives.

Not every opportunity bears a destiny seal of approval. Some opportunities are nothing more than potential distractions. Yet every golden opportunity is one-of-a-kind and meant just for you. These open doors are linked to your destiny code. They point to your purpose and they enable you to achieve it. Even the smallest of these opportunities is worthy of big attention.

When acted upon, opportunities are the gateways to your dream.

Opportunity 101

Every opportunity is unique, but all opportunities share common characteristics that will help you recognize a good one when it comes along.

Like threats, opportunities are external. They exist outside of you, yet they are always present. Whether or not you are aware of them, you are surrounded by situations and circumstances that exist to create increase in your life. This increase is not always immediately related to your finances. Increase can also be experienced in the social, physical, or spiritual aspects of life. In any case, opportunities for increase hold the promise of something better, greater, more fulfilling, or more rewarding.

Because opportunities are external, you cannot control how or when they will arise. However, you have complete jurisdiction over the way in which you respond to them. Your response will determine how much increase an opportunity will yield. In other words, there is an outcome or series of outcomes attached to every opportunity that comes your way. The character of those outcomes is directly tied to the nature of your response to the opportunity.

The first step in responding to an opportunity is to recognize its existence. Opportunities that lay dormant and untended yield no benefit. In fact, when opportunities consistently go unnoticed, the ground of your life space becomes fallow and resistant to yield. In the face of chronic inaction, overall outcomes are driven downward. Often we don't consciously acknowledge the reasons for the reversals we experience. This lack of observation further exacerbates the issue and can be very costly over the course of a lifetime.

Once your opportunity-detection skills are honed and you are able to spot life's golden opportunities, the *way* in which you respond becomes critical. Your approach to an externally occurring opportunity is determined by what is happening on the inside. The internal environment (the thought-life, internal belief structures, misbeliefs, fears, and any forms of unfinished business) governs all behavior and will also shape your critical responses to opportunity.

For instance, if you lack clarity because of lingering unmet needs and unresolved issues, you will find it hard to maintain the elevated perspective needed to be decisive. Instead you will have a tendency to hesitate or to forego action altogether. Likewise, if the fear of failure or rejection is what informs your approach, your negative expectations could lead you to procrastinate in the hope of avoiding emotional pain.

Unfortunately most opportunities have a limited shelf-life. They are connected with our destiny codes. We know these codes include entire systems of relationships and other connections working together to fulfill our life's purposes. The opportunities we encounter tend to be tied to the significant people and/or events (including emotional events) in our lives. All of these elements and life dynamics are fluid. The favorable set of circumstances that exists today may not be there tomorrow. Opportunity will not always "keep" for extended periods while we get ready to act.

Another important fact about opportunities: They travel hand in hand with threats making a passive approach unsuitable. Be watchful over the life space you occupy; the ground which surrounds your golden opportunities also contains some pitfalls. You can be blindsided by threats that go unnoticed. If that happens, the end result of a marvelous opportunity can be seriously compromised.

There's more than enough good news to go around however. Just as every opportunity is a gift that is tied to your purpose, every threat that is understood in the context of that purpose is also a gift. When you are faced with a threat (an obstacle, potential setback, or fear about either), be determined to mine its potential to make you stronger, smarter, more alert, and better prepared for your destiny.

As Joseph would attest, even your pain can leverage you to high places.

Use Awareness to Create Opportunity

When opportunity surrounds you and you desire to live strategically, conscious, intentional living is imperative. You'll remember from an earlier chapter that among our most fundamental skills are:

The ability to think.

The ability to act.

The ability to get results.

Your ability to think includes the function of awareness. This awareness involves being present to the moment and cognizant of the importance of what is going on around you.

Awareness is required in order to recognize and seize the opportunities that can lead to the fulfillment of your strategic life plan. This level of awareness is a hallmark of human existence. We are created to live and interact in fully conscious ways that make us part of the solution in every situation we encounter. This consciousness enables us to leverage the ability to think so that we are empowered to act. This in turn positions us to get results.

This awareness has a price however. That price is *the responsibility for what you know.* When you become aware of an opportunity, you also recognize its potential to produce gain. That potential benefit, like any other gift we receive, implies our responsibility for its appropriate use. An opportunity doesn't become a reality unless and until a human being makes the conscious choice to embrace it and act upon it.

This important choice can only be made within the context of your vision and with careful consideration to your mission, values, and priorities. Part of this consideration will determine whether or not the opportunity is aligned with your dream. Remember, not all opportunities are golden—some fall under the category of distractions. These may produce short-term gratification; but in the long run, they will drain your energy for the mission.

Since awareness of opportunity is the prerequisite to the taking of action, let's explore ways in which awareness can be diminished over the course of time. For some of us, life's difficulties and downturns have skewed our perspective in such a way as to dull our awareness of anything not directly related to the solving of the "crisis du jour." Too often adversity narrows our scope of vision to the point that we live (or more aptly, we *exist*) in survival mode. With our energy devoted to crisis management, we shut off the dream. If we're not careful, we can forget about the dream altogether.

Another awareness-killer is over reliance on outside factors. Many of us were raised to be overly dependent upon others. Some were over-protected as children or raised by parents whose own unmet needs fostered co-dependent behavior. As a result, we may have developed the expectation that someone else would handle or take blame for the issues in our lives. Therefore we excuse ourselves from being proactive and we fail to develop the acute sense of awareness that empowers us as adults.

Being challenged in the area of awareness needn't be a lifelong hindrance to achievement. Awareness can be cultivated by training or retraining your brain. Use your dream and the various elements of your strategic life plan as a target for your thought-life. When thoughts begin to scatter or when awareness fades, fix your mind on your purpose. Doing this as often as necessary will increase your level of awareness and intentionality and will empower you to aggressively activate the opportunities that await you.

The discovery and activation of opportunity is a creative process; your interaction with an opportunity releases the potential that is wrapped inside it and spawns future opportunities that are not yet visible to the naked eye.

Assess Opportunity Strategically

All opportunities are not created equal; therefore a well-developed ability to evaluate opportunities is central to the achievement of your desired outcomes. A simple and effective approach is to evaluate opportunities in much the same way that you would evaluate well-formed outcomes (see Chapter 5) and goals (see Chapter 9).

The basis of this evaluation is to examine each opportunity in the light of your strategic life plan and then decide whether the opportunity is moving in the direction of your dreams. Here are a few simple questions that will help you approach the assessment of opportunities strategically:

Does the opportunity dovetail with your purpose, i.e., with the things you want to achieve? The opportunities that serve your life's purpose will open doorways that lead to pathways; these pathways will in turn lead to your dream. There is always something destiny-related to be gained from an opportunity of this kind. The benefit could involve the development or improvement of a required skill or set of skills. For instance, if your dream is to be a journalist and a world-class journalist invites you into a mentoring relationship (and assuming no inappropriate motives are involved), you can expect to receive guidance and experience that will polish your skills and perhaps open additional doors of opportunity.

Why do you want to engage with this opportunity? When an opportunity opens up, ask yourself what makes it attractive to you. Make sure the "why" lines up with your purpose and is not inspired by any unmet needs or other forms of unfinished business. For instance, if a job opportunity seems attractive, check to be sure that it is really advancing your purpose and not just boosting a deflated ego. If you are seeking affirmation from a job title, you may enjoy that fleeting emotional high at the cost of your destiny fulfillment.

Is the opportunity in keeping with the terms and conditions (the cost) that you deem reasonable in the pursuit of your dream? You have already counted the cost of your dream. Likewise you'll want to be sure that every opportunity with which you engage is one to which you can commit wholeheartedly. If the opportunity comes at the cost of your overall ability to pursue your purpose in healthful, enriching, and beneficial ways, the opportunity may be suspect and will require further examination.

Can the opportunity be reasonably pursued—will reasonable methods and timeframes accomplish it, and are key factors related to the opportunity within your control? In order to successfully engage an opportunity, you will need to be able to develop a practical plan of approach. You will also need the assurance that you are not placing yourself at the mercy of factors which are entirely under the control of others. For instance, if your ability to benefit from an opportunity rests solely on whether or not another person performs in a diligent and timely manner, you may need to reconsider whether this opportunity is worth your while.

Does the opportunity promote intimacy through close, reciprocal relationships; does it engage your spirituality and promote generativity? Opportunities most often involve other people. Make certain that every opportunity invites honest, mutually beneficial interaction that is guided by integrity. Also be sure the opportunity lines up with your values, is meaningful, and is compatible with the spiritual side of your life. Finally, ask yourself whether the opportunity has the potential to produce results that affect others positively (perhaps to the extent that positive results achieved reach beyond your lifetime).

When you ask yourself these questions, the formulation of your answers will require more than a superficial level of awareness. At first glance some excellent opportunities may appear limited in scope or in their ability to meet your criteria. Yet it may be that the single opportunity being evaluated is merely a door-opener. Dig a little deeper to discern whether a seemingly insignificant opportunity is capable of generating future opportunities that meet your expectations.

Opportunity Patterns

Always evaluate opportunities within the larger context of your destiny code. Conversely, make it a point to become aware of patterns that emerge from the opportunities you encounter. These patterns often contain hints designed to enrich your understanding of your destiny code.

Forecast Opportunity's Seasons

Opportunities and seasons are dynamically linked: Changing seasons give way to new opportunities and new opportunities can usher in new seasons. If you keep these dynamics in mind, you will be better equipped to accurately identify both your seasons and the golden opportunities that come your way. Let's consider the connection between certain types of seasons and the opportunities linked to them. (See Chapter 4 for more information about the seasons of life.)

Seasons of closed doors. When a favorable situation begins to turn and you find yourself running into one closed door after another, it is often an indication that a new season is beginning. If you keep a clear head by refusing to drag unfinished business from one season to another, you will be positioned to spot the opportunities that accompany these destiny-related shifts in momentum. These may include new locations, new associations, and new circumstances that reveal new open doors to your dream.

Seasons of relational shifts. Certain relationships in our lives have limited life cycles. When these cycles have run their course, the relationship wanes. Often this is painful to us and to others so we attempt to resuscitate the relationship when it would be wiser to let it go. Some of our relationships wane so that new destiny-driven relationships can flourish; the winding down of a relationship can become a golden opportunity to invest in new associations and the open doors they bring.

Seasons of relational shift also include painful seasons of rejection. Amazingly enough these painful times provide us with unexpected opportunities to grow stronger, know ourselves better, become more compassionate, and learn to lead more wisely.

Seasons of changing needs and desires. As we continue to grow emotionally, professionally, socially, spiritually, and financially, we move through phases of life in which our needs and desires change. When these needs and desires are destiny-driven, they compel us to seek after something more. This seeking, when done in earnest and with healthy motives, will cause us to uncover previously unknown realms of opportunity, which will in turn lead us into new seasons.

Seasons of constriction (or even disgust). When a healthy pattern of growth produces changing needs and desires, we feel confined to spaces and functions that are limiting to the pursuit of destiny. These seasons are opportunities to break out of self-limiting paradigms and look outside the box. During these transitions, we often become more adventuresome and more willing to take risks. In this dynamic state we tend to turn over every stone (metaphorically speaking), and we tend to find opportunity everywhere we look. If acted upon, these opportunities will release us into new seasons of freedom and fulfillment.

> "Trouble is only opportunity in work clothes."[3]
> —Henry J. Kaiser, American industrialist

Included in seasons of constriction are the seasons in which we redefine ourselves. These are the times in which our paradigms are so shattered by progress or crisis that we are forced into what I call "the hallway of the unknown." That is the uncomfortable place where we are invited to let go of the status quo and enter into the greatness for which we are destined.

Finally, when assessing opportunities, take a hint from the trajectories along which these opportunities travel. Be able to recognize whether the path of opportunity leads upward or downward—into new places of advancement or backward to old, ill-fitting paradigms. There is no such thing as standing still: Any opportunity that does not lead you forward will surely set you back.

Forward is the chosen direction of those who live strategically. Go for it, and remember that a single opportunity can catapult you into an exciting new season.

Take a Closer Look at Your Crises

> "In the Chinese language, the word *crisis* is composed of two characters that are placed together. One means 'danger,' and the other means 'opportunity.'"[4]

Hit a Crisis, Discover an Opportunity

Threats against your dream need never be fatal. They are simply opportunities of a different stripe. Therefore they are prime opportunities for growth. There is a story told about a family man who lost his job as a truck driver. At the time, trucking jobs were scarce and unemployed truckers were many.

Distressed and fearful of what an interruption in income would mean to his family, the man scrambled to find another job. He filed application after application to no avail. Finally he was granted an interview by his only remaining prospect. Early in the conversation, the employer asked the man whether he had any computer skills.

"No," the man responded. "I've been driving trucks for fifteen years and have never used a computer."

"Sorry, we only hire drivers with computer skills," was the interviewer's curt response.

Desperate for the job, the man pleaded, "I'm the best truck driver out there and I'm a quick study, too. If you'll give me a shot at this job, I'll learn to use a computer in no time."

With no shortage of applicants from which to choose, the employer stood his ground. The disappointed man left the interview and wandered the streets in despair. With nothing but a five-dollar bill to his name, he worried about the fate of his family.

With fear gripping his heart and nothing left to lose, the man took the crumpled bill and purchased some oranges from a grocery store. He then stationed himself on a busy street corner and sold one orange at a time to lunch-hour pedestrians. In a short while, the man had sold out his entire inventory—at a profit!

Excited by his success, he repeated the process and amassed a few more precious dollars. Recognizing the potential, he returned day after day and went from selling a few pieces of fruit to selling truckloads full.

In a few short years, the enterprise had grown exponentially. The former truck driver took his financial gain, added to it his understanding of the trucking business, and founded what would become a multi-million dollar produce business.

The once-dejected truck driver was thankful for the way things had worked out. After all, if he had not been turned down for the driver's job he wanted so badly, he might never have ventured outside the box of his limited experience to do something new.

Still it was the way in which he approached his crisis that led to the full flowering of the unusual opportunity that existed right under his nose. How many people accustomed to a decent hourly wage would even consider selling pieces of fruit on a street corner—especially at the rate of just a few cents profit per sale!

Regardless of how your opportunity originates, it is your response that translates the growth potential it offers into realized increase. The important fact to remember is that all opportunities, even crises, are potential growth opportunities.

The Wheel of Opportunity

Every opportunity leads to an outcome. Every outcome, whether pleasing or disappointing, opens the door to yet another opportunity and another chance to take great strides in the direction of your dream.

Leave Nothing on the Table

Opportunities come in many forms. Your vision is itself an opportunity waiting to be explored and exploited in the pursuit of your purpose. Ideas—for inventions or products, songs or stories, logos or word plays— are opportunities. Take your ideas to heart. Write them down. Do something with them because they are priceless!

Remember that destiny supersedes finite thinking. Be open to those opportunities that may be different from what you had in mind. Stay perched in your watchtower so that your perspective is always elevated. Opportunities are more easily discovered and appraised from higher ground.

Refuse to forfeit the rewards of destiny fulfillment. Resist the urge to grumble at the responsibility that is attached to the golden opportunities that come your way. If an opportunity supports your strategic life plan, you have already counted its cost to be fair and reasonable. Pay the price with the joy of expectation in your heart reminding you of the wonderful outcomes that are ahead.

Prize each destiny-laden opportunity for the potential it contains. Realize that this potential is bigger than any threat or obstacle that stands before you...and it can take you into the destiny realms for which you long.

Now, turn the page and discover within yourself the ability to transform possibility into *probability*.

12

TRANSFORM POSSIBILITY
INTO PROBABILITY

David Frost reportedly shared an inspiring story of perseverance involving American businessman, Ross Perot. It seems that Perot embarked on a personal mission of service during the bitter days of the Vietnam War. Perot's goal was to send a Christmas present to every prisoner of war held by the North Vietnamese.

With a hired fleet of jetliners poised to make the delivery, thousands of gifts were wrapped and readied for shipment. But getting the convoy into Hanoi would not be easy. The war was fully engaged and American B-52s were bombing Vietnamese targets. Boeing 707s, even those loaded with gifts for POWs, were unwelcome in the embattled nation.

Determined to turn an opportunity to serve others into a mission accomplished, Perot made the Vietnamese a stunning offer. In exchange for their permission to fly gifts into Hanoi, he would send a construction firm to Vietnam to rebuild any structures damaged by American bombing raids.

Unmoved by Perot's creative and generous attempt at compromise, the Vietnamese rejected his proposal. Christmas was nearing and time was running out for a holiday delivery. The specially wrapped presents, designed to bring cheer to POWs held in squalor far from home, were hopelessly tied up in red tape.

Yet Perot didn't quit. He believed the mission was meaningful and the timing of the opportunity was right. He dropped his stymied plan and flew into Moscow, air fleet and shipment in tow. From the Soviet capital, Perot's aides mailed the presents, one by one, to Hanoi. Happily, the gifts were received intact and POWs enjoyed an interlude of holiday cheer.[1]

Perot, who is now counted among the world's billionaires, knows how to get things done. He has a well-practiced resolve and an unrelenting grasp on the methods of turning an opportunity—a *possibility* that exists in the theoretical realm—into a *probability*, that is, something that is primed to become a reality.

Not every opportunity is as logistically loaded as Ross Perot's mission was. Still, when it comes to achieving desired outcomes, there are days when the gulf between possibility and probability seems perilously wide. The gap is often bridged with little more than a manageable, common-sense approach involving attitudes and behaviors. When these rudiments are undertaken consistently, the odds can swing powerfully in your favor, without breaking the bank or risking burnout.

> Opportunity is missed by most people because it is dressed in overalls and looks like work.[2] —Thomas A. Edison

Begin at the End

The vision of your completed dream bridges another important span— the gulf between present and future—and in some ways erases the distinctions between the two. With your vision established, your thought-life places you at the end of the story so that in a sense your dream must catch up with you. The choices you make in support of your desired end result enable it to do just that.

Let's walk through a practical illustration of this time-traversing process. You'll remember that an architect starts with the big picture which is the vision of the completed structure and experiences the building which, at that stage, exists only in the architect's mind. Once the vision is framed, the architect is ready to develop a finely detailed blueprint. Notice that the blueprint is not begun until the end result is firmly established in the designer's mind.

Once the blueprint is completed, it guides the builders through hundreds, if not thousands, of minute steps. These steps lead the process forward to the completion of the desired end result, but they do so only by referring *back* to the vision (which was created in *the past* as a picture of *the future*). The past and future meet when construction is complete. At that point the building is more than an idea affixed to a document, it is a reality occupying physical space and performing its purpose in real time.

These dynamics apply not only to life design, but also to your interaction with opportunities. When a single, destiny-related opportunity is undertaken, it is a microcosm of your overall strategic life plan: it supports your vision; it reflects your unique factor and signature style; and it is compatible with your strategies, tactics, and goals.

Your response to an opportunity has great bearing on the degree to which your strategic life plan is realized. Therefore be sure to develop in your mind a clear picture of where you see the opportunity taking you—before you act. *Seeing* the opportunity brought to fruition is an important dynamic in the shift from possibility to probability.

Of course, you can't perceive every layer and aspect of an opportunity at the outset, but you can get a sense of the potential it holds. Then you can use your power of choice to bridge the span between present and future by planning your actions backward from the final outcome. At that point, you are prepared to create a blueprint—your strategic plan to exploit the opportunity effectively and in mutually beneficial ways.

This blueprint is your script. It is an important part of the proactive development of opportunities encountered en route to your dream. If scripting your approach to opportunities seems like a daunting task, be encouraged. You won't need to reinvent the wheel or concoct complex new approaches to every possibility that exists in your life space. Instead, you can refer to the handbook you've already created—your strategic life plan. When responding to opportunities you consider to be aligned with your purpose, use the well-considered elements of that plan to guide your decisions and actions.

To effectively turn possibility (opportunity) into probability and to do so without compromising your overall mission and well-being, be willing to uncover any conflicts between your strategic life plan and any opportunity that arises. Opportunities, even those that are ill-advised, can be alluring because they speak of something new. They titillate the senses and appeal to our emotions and impulses, including those inclinations still governed by unmet needs.

Be sure that your assessment of opportunities is reasoned and not overly emotional. Don't be guided by the adrenalin and affirmation an opportunity suggests, but by how well-matched the opportunity is to the purpose at hand. By holding the opportunity up to the light of your strategic life plan, you will avoid costly diversions from your mission.

Your strategic life plan will also help you gauge the appropriate intensity of your response to individual opportunities. The amount of energy and resources devoted to any activity should be in keeping with your previously made assessment of what you believe to be the reasonable cost of your dream. Remember that the total price you are willing to pay will be thrown out of balance if you over-commit in any one area. Therefore it is important to respond to opportunity in a measured fashion. Avoid bankrupting your energy and resource pool prematurely by managing your expectations and your energy output with care.

Ride the Opportunity Time Machine

Study the following example of working backward from the vision of your intended outcome and making the most of opportunities along the way. As you read, consider the ways in which this model resembles or differs from your experience with a current or past opportunity. Jot down any notes that will be helpful in producing better outcomes.

From the beginning, you envision your desired end result. Your vision is to build a particular style of log cabin in a specific type of setting. The cabin will be situated on an expansive, wooded lot and it will be constructed with logs hewn from the indigenous trees growing on the lot. Your vision describes the possibility of something in the future which, for now, exists only in the theoretical.

In the gap between present and future, you devise and implement a strategy, and you make the most of the opportunities that are aligned with your vision. One of the ways in which you promote the chances of your possibility becoming probable is by reducing unnecessary spending. This is freeing up the cash you need to set aside for the vision.

You are also watching and studying the real estate market and actively seeking opportunities in the form of acreage that meet your criteria. You are becoming better informed about wooded properties and better equipped to select the right lot.

When the right property becomes available, you will recognize it; and because you have been saving money over time, you will be able to maximize the golden opportunity to purchase the ideal lot. As you continue to follow through on your strategy, your possibility is becoming more and more probable.

Eventually, past and future meet as your previously charted vision of the future becomes reality. Months or years have passed, the necessary amount of money has been accumulated, and your diligent search for land has yielded results. You find the perfect property populated by thousands of strong trees. The lot satisfies your previously set criteria and will accommodate the log cabin you've had in mind from the beginning. Your vision has spawned another opportunity—to purchase the land and build a cabin.

With the deed signed, you clear the section of land needed to accommodate the structure and cut down additional trees as needed to provide enough lumber for the cabin and to create an environmentally sound, useable lot. From a tactical standpoint, your tools include an axe and other implements, plus the "elbow grease" needed to get the job done. You have moved beyond the stage of what is theoretically possible. You are now in the place where probability can soon become reality.

Completing your mission at this point is a simple matter of seeing your plan through to the end. If you do this, your vision from long ago will fully materialize and you will have your long awaited log cabin set in the woods.

These steps are so logical that we easily give mental assent to them. Yet we need to do more than agree with a good plan. In the midst of the demands of our active lives, we have to *contend* for the vision. If we don't, the plan will slip little by little until we find ourselves utterly unprepared to engage opportunity when it arrives. Before you move on, consider the notes you've made and ask yourself how this model might be helpful to you in the future.

POSSIBILITY	PROBABILITY	REALITY
A FUTURE PROSPECT OR POTENTIAL; CAPABILITY OF EXISTING OR HAPPENING OR BEING TRUE; "THERE IS A POSSIBILITY THAT HIS SENSE OF SMELL HAS BEEN IMPAIRED"[3]	A MEASURE OF HOW LIKELY IT IS THAT SOME EVEN WILL OCCUR[4]	THE STATE OF BEING ACTUAL OR REAL[5]

You've Gotta Believe

Opportunities become probabilities when they are seized *and* acted upon. In the end-from-the-beginning example, the vision inspired the person to action whose dream it was to build a log cabin. Opportunities were seized and acted upon consistently until the dream became a physical reality.

Few things are more rewarding than a dream fulfilled, but truth be told, the landscape of the average life is littered with the rubble of *un*fulfilled dreams. There are many reasons for that sad fact. We'll use our log cabin illustration to illustrate one of them.

We saw how the actions taken in the log cabin example maximized opportunity; but actions alone did not get the job done. There is a missing ingredient that completes this recipe for success; that ingredient is *belief.* We discussed belief briefly in Chapter 8. Let's take a closer look at how belief works in general and specifically in regard to opportunity.

For starters, beliefs about belief vary widely. To many people, belief as a component of success sounds too ethereal to be meaningful. I would suggest otherwise and offer this observation: Although belief is seen as an intangible, it is substantial. I have seen in my personal experience and in my tenure as a life coach that belief is the very substance of one's dreams. It is the glue that binds together emotions, actions, and resources to create something out of what seems to be nothing.

But belief is not an attitude that is bestowed—and it is not the exclusive domain of the fortunate. Belief is a human experience that is, first and foremost, a choice. When faced with an idea or any other opportunity, you must choose to believe in it. Belief will motivate you to pursue opportunity because you *believe* the opportunity has merit and promise.

In the case of the log cabin anecdote, our dreamer had a vision and an obvious and intentional belief in that vision. This belief created the emotional environment in which the dreamer was empowered to create and follow a strategic plan. Without this underpinning of belief, the vision would have died the silent death of a passing thought.

That is precisely why belief is so important. We already know that *attitudes drive behavior*. Belief in your dream is an attitude—it produces expectation and drives behavior that is in line with your dream. More than any other action taken or choice made, belief is the element that will bring your dream to fruition.

Belief in an opportunity works the same way. Here's how the process functions:

>*Belief applied to an idea or other opportunity produces possibility.*
>
>*Belief applied to possibility produces a plan that makes the possible probable.*
>
>*Belief applied to what is probable keeps the vision alive so that probability becomes reality.*

Belief is an important and necessary ingredient in any pursuit, especially when you are pursuing something that does not yet exist and/or cannot be seen with the physical eye. Some opportunities seem unimaginable when considered in the light of traditional thought. These are the ideas or scenarios we would be hard-pressed to prove to skeptics (or even ourselves) because they are outside the box of common knowledge and often have no known precedent to substantiate them.

Therefore we have to *believe* in order to proceed. Belief creates the emotional environment that supports the passionate pursuit of the opportunity before us. With belief in play, we consistently and fervently act until the opportunity has been successfully exploited. In time the unseen will become tangible, and faith will no longer be needed because the reality will be standing right in front of us. But without belief in the operation at the outset, there would be no reason to proceed and no resilience to persevere in the face of opposition.

Belief is the glue that holds your dreams and opportunities together—and it is the substance that bridges the gap between opportunity and probability.

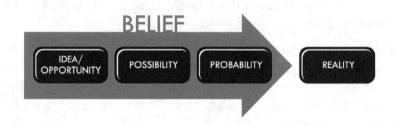

Supersize the Positive

A balanced approach will go a long way in transforming possibility into probability. On the one hand, it is important to avoid overly emotional responses that focus too heavily on the excitement an opportunity offers. At the same time, it is essential that we stay in tune to the upside of every opportunity *and* to the power we have to transform the landscape of our lives. We'll focus on three areas in particular.

Your power to convert opportunity into probability. Even the best of opportunities cannot boast of 100 percent upside. Therefore, your perspective regarding the drawbacks or imperfections associated with each case is critical. In the end, your view of the downside issues will be more of a determining factor than the issues themselves.

Interestingly, those who face the most challenges are often those who make the most of opportunities. It is a story we Americans see repeated over and over again: Those who are born in what the rest of the world aptly calls the *Land of Opportunity* sometimes take it for granted. Meanwhile, those who struggle for years to come to America do so because they value the opportunities that exist here and plan to capitalize on what the United States has to offer.

An American-born woman who worked as a receptionist in a nursing home told the amazing story of a Honduran couple who immigrated to the United States. Apparently the pair came from a poor town in Honduras where each of them had large, poverty-stricken families. Neither husband nor wife was educated. The only jobs open to them were the kinds of jobs most Americans would describe as menial.

The husband worked as a janitor in the nursing home and his wife worked as an aide whose primary responsibilities were to change linens and bedpans. In a facility staffed by several clerical workers and a large number of professionals including nurses, doctors, occupational therapists, accountants, and social workers, the positions held by the Honduran couple were among the lowest-paying in the organization.

Still, both husband and wife were thankful for their jobs and for the earning power they enjoyed in the United States. They regularly sent money to help their families in Honduras and contributed to a savings account with small dollar amounts set aside out of every paycheck. In just a few years, they used their savings to purchase a small, distressed property which they renovated themselves and leased to tenants.

The pair held onto their jobs and continued to assist their loved ones in Honduras. They also continued to save. After six short years in the United States, they had purchased, renovated, and rented out six buildings, one of which was a multi-family dwelling! By this time, the couple's monthly income exceeded that of the American-born non-professional staffers at the nursing home—as did their net worth in most cases.

Part of the personal power these hard-working immigrants harnessed had to do with their optimistic attitude and their refusal to make excuses. Working five and sometimes six days a week at manual labor might have been seen by some of their co-workers as a good reason *not* to renovate buildings on their remaining days off.

Yet this industrious couple saw things differently. They had come to America believing that opportunity was there for the asking. They proved their belief true by uncovering opportunity all around them and by super-sizing the upside of every situation. They looked each opportunity in the eye and said, "I will do whatever is necessary to turn this possibility into a probability. I *will* achieve my dream."

The role of your thought-life in converting opportunity into probability. The willingness of the Honduran couple to use their personal power in approaching opportunity was birthed in their thought-life. They believed unswervingly in their mission and they were convinced of their ability to complete it.

They faced many obstacles, including the lack of education and expertise. In addition their English was poor which made communication and negotiations difficult. They could have succumbed to discouragement. Instead, they refused to be governed by negative thoughts and temporary obstacles.

They learned that when niggling thoughts of discouragement or weariness creep in, they have to be tackled. Instead of burying their heads in the sand, they returned to the watchtower and took another look at the big picture. From higher ground their viewpoint of the opportunity was refreshed. They responded to negative thoughts with bigger, more productive thoughts about the benefits of sticking with their efforts. Every time they supersized the positive, they increased their chances of success.

The power of potential to overcome obstacles and produce increased probability. The power of potential wrapped within your opportunity is always greater than the power of the obstacles to offset it. The idea is to keep your eyes fixed on the potential so that you don't surrender to an obstacle that has little real ability to thwart success.

Suppose that you have a shipment of goods that you know will produce an outstanding profit margin once the goods are sold. Now assume that you have hit one transport challenge after another including severe weather, the withdrawal of a shipping bid, and a change in shipping law that affects your load.

As the challenges pile up, you may feel overwhelmed by the weight of them. You'll need to find a new shipper, reroute the goods around the weather, and address the compliance issues that have changed unexpectedly. All of this will take time and energy and will likely impact your bottom line.

Still, because of the potential linked to this opportunity, the end result is worthy of your efforts to overcome the setbacks. If you stick with your mission, this sales opportunity will result in a net gain to your bottom line and may open the door to future opportunities as yet unseen.

Supersizing the positive will help you get the most out of every opportunity. It will also keep your perspective and your spirits elevated making the journey more enjoyable.

Stack the Deck in Your Favor

While stacking the deck is dishonorable in a card game, doing everything you can within legal and moral means to enhance your chances of success is the honorable thing to do. When faced with an opportunity that is consistent with your destiny, you can adjust your positioning as you go and increase your chances of converting the opportunity before you into a reality.

Recognize your right of seizure. When opportunity knocks, you have every right to seize it. Check your posture. Are you standing on the balls of your feet, ready to grasp the opportunity with both hands? Or were you caught resting on your heels or even wondering whether or not you qualify to accept your opportunity delivery?

Our responses to opportunity most often rest somewhere between these two extremes. Be aware of your posture the moment opportunity strikes. Be sure to square your shoulders, establish your footing, and remind yourself that the opportunity is yours to seize.

Regardless of past failures or disappointments, you are worthy of every opportunity that is related to your destiny code. You needn't seek the approval of others. Some may bristle at your good fortune; they may even try to take you down a peg. Others will want to convince you that the opportunity is over your head. Some may even mock you or attempt to diminish the value of the opportunity. Learn to recognize envy when you see it. Dismiss any naysayers whose motives are not pure. None of them will pay the price of the destiny opportunities you lose on the basis of their misguided or ill-intentioned advice.

Be decisive and strongly intentional. Don't procrastinate in the face of an opportunity. Procrastination extinguishes purpose by creating a backlog of unfinished business that clutters your mind. And remember—open doors don't stay open indefinitely. Your opportunity has a shelf life that is tied to your destiny code and to the relationships and timelines that are part of that code.

Remain decisive and avoid procrastination by breaking the opportunity up into manageable pieces. Progress is incremental anyway, so taking one step at a time is a wise approach. Sort out the steps that need to be placed on the front burner and focus on those first. With progress underway, the task list will be less overwhelming. Before you know it, you'll be heading down the other side of the mountain.

Intentionality is the trait of decisive people. Never lose sight of the underlying purpose of the opportunities you encounter. If you feel yourself losing perspective, ask yourself two questions: *Why here?* and *Why now?* This will help you maintain a strong sense of intentionality that is based in the knowledge of your mission and a clear understanding of how the current opportunity facilitates that mission.

Deny the comfort zone. You can improve your ability to convert destiny-driven, well-timed opportunities by refusing the safety of the comfort zone. Remember that opportunities prefer an outside-the-box climate. If you want to be where the opportunities are, avoid the comfort zone—*always.* And while you're navigating the process of opportunity conversion, keep a fresh supply of outside-the-box approaches at the ready.

Distinguish ripe opportunities from those not yet ready for harvest. Sometimes an opportunity that seems perfectly aligned with your purpose shows up at the wrong time. Unless you are disciplined enough to refrain from investing in a poorly-timed opportunity, you may forego some of the benefits the same opportunity would have afforded you later on.

If you've ever sunk your teeth into an unripe peach, you know how disappointing it can be. After being surprised by the lack of flavor and unpleasant texture, you wish you'd never tasted the fruit at all. The opportunity to enjoy a luscious, satisfying taste experience was wasted because the timing was off.

The same is true of an ill-timed opportunity. To avoid the pitfalls of poor timing, assess your opportunities carefully with your strategic life plan as your guide. By taking a measured approach, you can eliminate misfires and save yourself the unnecessary hardship of wasted energy and resources.

There's one more foundational way to stack the destiny deck in your favor . . . but that's a topic for another chapter—the next one!

13

STOP SOLVING PROBLEMS AND START CREATING SOLUTIONS

*Creativity can solve almost any problem. The creative act, the defeat of
habit by originality, overcomes everything.[1]* —George Lois

George Lois is an innovator, a giant of advertising and communications
whose stunning work has rejuvenated besieged businesses and revital-
ized well-known brands. With an unforgettable image or a brilliant turn of
phrase, George Lois has demonstrated his ability to turn the tide in business
and culture and produce something of value out of nothing but imagination.

In Lois's business, creativity is the coin of the realm, the supreme problem solver. Yet it can be argued that the creative power of Lois's imagination does more than solve marketing problems. His is the kind of mind that
creates solutions. His inspired innovations not only address challenges, they
change the game altogether.

Lois has done it over and over again with credits too numerous to
mention. But a single sentence from his online bio recounts two of them,
saying that Lois "made a failing MTV a huge success with his 'I Want My
MTV' campaign . . . [and] created a new marketing category, Gourmet
Frozen Foods, with his name Lean Cuisine."[2]

You don't have to be a fan of MTV or Lean Cuisine to realize the
potency of imagination revealed in these examples. The impact of

creative solutions on the collective consciousness is immediately apparent. It speaks of the kind of paradigm-busting prowess described by 20th-century Irish short story writer Sean O'Faolain as "imagination that is so intense that it creates a new reality...it makes things happen."[3]

The ability to generate a *new reality* is what distinguishes the creation of solutions from the mere solving of problems. While the practice of problem solving is restricted to the confines of an existing paradigm and the use of available materials, the art of creating solutions is not bound by these limitations. It takes place outside the box and accomplishes more than fixing what is broken. This is key because problems rarely stand alone. When one shows up, it is often symptomatic of a larger issue involving the paradigm itself. This is particularly true of persistent problems and recurring patterns of struggle.

Problem solving falls short in these situations because it rivets our attention on the problem instead of the context in which it was formed. When beset by a pressing issue, we become familiar with its mechanics and we bemoan its unnerving side effects. Desperate for relief, we reach for hammer, nails, and masking tape. We try to cobble together the fractured pieces of the situation, hoping against hope that the fix will hold. Then we return to business as usual knowing deep down that the problem will inevitably rear its head at some future date.

The process for creating solutions is not designed to restore business as usual. It is all about reaching a new level of business as *un*usual. Solution creation is not a limiting function; instead, it dissolves boundaries and opens the door to increased opportunity. Solution creation is not an accidental activity; it requires us to look beyond the problem and carefully inspect the paradigms within which the problem was birthed.

Solution creators realize that patches don't work. They know that old paradigms can't solve problems—they can only perpetuate them. And they understand that problem solving can never really move you forward. In fact, it will most likely mire you in the past.

"An idea is salvation by imagination."[4] —Frank Lloyd Wright

Solution Creation Brings Transformation

In his *New York Magazine* article "Candidate.com," Michael Wolff discusses the presidential candidacy of Howard Dean who was contending for the nomination of the Democratic Party at the time the article was written in 2003.

The article describes what was then considered a revolutionary solution created by the Dean campaign to answer an old problem—how to raise more funds than your opponent.

In the high stakes game of politics, the competition is stiff and every dollar counts. In 2003 every candidate was competing in all of the traditional fundraising forums. One of the standard tools was direct mail which, according to Wolff, was first used as a campaign fundraising tool by George McGovern in 1970. But the direct mail option was wearing thin: McGovern's rate of response to direct mail in the 1970s was a healthy four percent while in 2003, one half of one percent was the norm.[5]

The Dean campaign sought a solution that would turn the numbers inside out. They went directly to the grass roots, the growing number of citizens sitting on the other side of the computer monitor.

To their delight the experiment paid off. What they discovered was a virtually untapped source of motivated givers. We have learned since that although many Internet contributors give in limited amounts, many of them give repeatedly. Michael Wolff recognized the outside-the-box flavor of Dean's approach and he described the power of the newly created solution to make Dean's candidacy financially viable:

> The Dean campaign, everyone knows, has been made possible by the Internet. The campaign is a pure response-rate phenomenon. By being the first presidential candidate to deftly and efficiently access interest groups assembled through the Internet . . . Dean has assembled a financing basis that threatens to swamp his competitors.
>
> The campaign has even made its ability to instantly raise money through its Internet method something of a sporting event. On occasions when the president has held one of his

fabled (and traditional) many-thousands-a-plate dinners, the Dean campaign has accepted the challenge and raised as much with an Internet plea.

The Internet—which has still not revealed how it will ever reliably produce profits for the commercial sector—turns out to be a remarkable political money machine.[6]

That's the overwhelming power of solution creation. It changes the dynamics within an existing paradigm to the point that the paradigm must give way to a new reality. A truly creative solution comes from someone willing to test a unique mindset. The solution in turn creates a new mindset for everyone it touches.

Whatever your political viewpoint, there is no doubt that Dean's team was the first to test this innovation on such a scale. They weren't trying to tweak an existing method such as direct mail; they realized the times had changed. They knew there wasn't a Band-Aid big enough to make the old ways work in today's world. They left the past behind and created a solution they believed was compatible with their vision. And they got everybody's attention. Today the method they pioneered has become standard and continues to produce extraordinary results.

Think the Way a Solution Creator Thinks

Solution creation is not for those who prefer the safety of inside-the-box living—it is for people like you, people committed to the practice of strategic living and unwilling to settle for temporary fixes and duct-tape remedies.

Solution creation takes you from "making do" to "making new." It is what George Lois called "the defeat of habit by originality" and it has the capacity to "overcome everything."[7] It is anything but a reflex action; it requires active participation, awareness, thoughtfulness, and a balanced approach to risk tolerance.

There are certain common traits shared by solution creators. Following are five of these qualities, as contrasted to an inside-the-box, problem-solving approach:

Solution creators focus on the possibilities rather than on the problems. When a difficulty arises, the human tendency is to develop a laser-beam focus on the problem and the brutal details of its downside. The problem-solving viewpoint assumes that the realm of possibility is automatically diminished by the presence of a challenge. Therefore choices are perceived to be more limited than before the problem arrived. Not surprisingly, the problem-solver feels caught between a rock and a hard place.

On the other hand, an elevated perspective affords the solution creator a panoramic view of the new possibilities every problem spawns. The solution creator realizes that the problem has produced possibilities that didn't exist before the difficulty began. Instead these possibilities arose *because* of the problem. They include the opportunity...

- To see the situation from a less habitual and more productive perspective.

- To respond to a recurring problem in a new way designed to produce a new outcome.

- To deal with the "root" rather than the "fruit" of an issue.

- To see another's point of view and uncover previously unrecognized win/win solutions.

Solution creators don't like dark clouds hovering over them any more than problem solvers do. What sets them apart from everyone else is their fierce determination to turn the situation around by uncovering the cloud's silver lining.

Solution-creating example: The somewhat exasperated parent of a hyperactive child endeavors to discover the source of the child's restless state. Regardless of whether the child's behavior is the result of attention deficit disorder or some other cause, the parent is empowered by the information gathered.

With a better understanding of *why* the child is hyperactive, the parent is better able to respond to the challenge in productive ways and finds it easier to avoid responses of annoyance or embarrassment for the child's unusual behavior.

This proactive parent recognizes an opportunity to match the child's energy level with a previously unexplored interest or passion, in this case an affinity for music.

The parent creates a home environment which allows this predisposition to be nurtured. As a result the child has a productive outlet for the boundless energy that once seemed so troublesome. The child benefits from the newfound pursuit and becomes increasing passionate about it. With the parent's help, the child has discovered new meaning and fulfillment...and possibly a purpose in life.

Solution creators embrace the present moment to create what never existed. Often when problems occur, we see them as interruptions to our well-intentioned plans. When these interruptions occur, we set aside our forward-looking activities and wait for the storm to pass. There is a fallacy in this approach, and it has wide-reaching implications: there is no such thing as a problem-free existence, and if we allow problems to shut us down, we might as well be content to live in shut-down mode indefinitely.

Solution creators expect problems to be part and parcel of their progress toward destiny achievement. They don't stop the presses every time something goes wrong or something else fails to go right. They see problems as opportunities in disguise. You'll remember the words of Thomas Edison, a man familiar with solution creation; he said these opportunities are often missed because they are "dressed in overalls and [look] like work."[8]

Solution creators learn to appreciate every moment in life including the challenging ones. In good times and bad, they stay on track; as a result they learn the valuable art of converting problems into the promise of something that did not exist. Although he was one of the world's most prolific and influential inventors, Thomas Edison experienced thousands of failures—and saw every one of them as keys to his eventual success.

> Solution-creating example: An early middle-aged woman is tragically and unexpectedly widowed when her husband suffers a massive heart attack. After forty years of marriage and two blissful years of retirement, the pair had become inseparable. They shared many common interests and had little need for the company of others.

The wife is heartbroken at her loss. With their joint retirement plan scuttled, she feels disoriented and without purpose. Yet she notices that the pain of her own heartbreak has made her more sensitive to the needs of others.

She realizes that this difficult season has the potential to break her or make her a better person so she decides to find a productive outlet for her increased compassion. She applies as a volunteer to assist those trying to cope with the suicide of a loved one. Seeing a great need in her community, she eventually organizes a support group and begins planning events to help grieving people reconnect with life. In the process her own grief is healed and her joy for living returns.

Solution creators use problems (and other negative outcomes) to set them free from old limitations. Inside-the-box living encourages us to ignore pain and sweep important issues under the rug. As long as we run from situations we don't understand and continue to live in denial, our problems become more entrenched. They increase in their power to control us and they impose ever more stringent, destiny-disabling limitations upon us.

Solution creators allow life's pain and problems to churn the waters of life and bring any unfinished business to the surface. Instead of running from the mess, they expose it to the light. Therefore they are able to purge any relational, emotional, financial, or professional impurities from their lives. They become increasingly well-balanced so that goals, vision, and values are in sync and they are free from external and internal limitations and more prone to fulfilling their destinies.

Solution-creating example: A young man with excellent skills and education is unexpectedly laid off from his job. Although he was not the only person released by the company, he is devastated by a sense of rejection and he is ashamed to tell friends and loved ones that he is jobless.

The man remembers having experienced similar emotional turmoil as a teenager jilted by his girlfriend. At the time, he saved face by telling friends and family that he had ended the relationship. Now ten years later he recognizes a pattern and the presence of unfinished emotional business. He is eager to deal with it head on; he acknowledges the pain of rejection and seeks to uproot any misbeliefs attached to it.

He comes to realize that his identity has been based in performance. The resulting insecurity and neediness have adversely affected his job behaviors. Whether or not these behaviors resulted in his being laid off, he feels empowered by the development of a healthier self-image that is based in his *being* rather than his *doing*.

He reexamines his goals and flags those that were tied to his need for affirmation. He approaches his job search with a renewed sense of purpose and self-confidence and finds a much more fulfilling job than the one he lost. Because he approaches his work from an elevated perspective, both his emotional state and performance improve.

Solution creators don't wait to be rescued by others; instead, they see themselves as resourceful—able to think, act, and get results in every situation. One-hundred percent of the world's population throughout history has been stricken by trouble of some kind. In the absence of an elevated perspective, these setbacks can cause us to feel vulnerable and inadequate. Often we see the problems as being bigger than our capacity to overcome them. For many, this heightened sense of vulnerability triggers the subliminal desire to be rescued from the situation. This is a paralyzing form of survival mode in which there is a tendency to take no action at all. Therefore the problem gets bigger.

Solution creators do not become passive, but proactive, in the face of trouble. They waste neither time nor energy hoping that someone will save them. They don't see themselves as victims but as soon-to-be victors. They believe they are better able than anyone to create the specific solutions they need in life. This clarity is generated in part because proactive people make it a practice to put unfinished business to rest.

Solution-creating example: A young married woman who is a stay-at-home mom learns that her husband has been arrested for a white-collar crime and stands a good chance of doing significant jail time. With his trial just three months away, she realizes that she may soon be without an income.

Other than her excellent parenting and homemaking abilities, she lacks the skills and experience to find a job that will cover childcare costs and household expenses. She considers waiting to see what happens with her husband's trial; if it were to go badly, she could take the baby and move back home with her parents.

Instead she decides to take a proactive approach and provide daycare for the children of single and working moms. She spreads the word among her friends and places her ad on every available community bulletin board.

Later her husband is convicted and receives a five-year sentence. However, by the time he is remanded to prison, she has a house full of children to care for daily. She enjoys her work and earns enough money to support the family. Both she and her child benefit from being able to stay in their home, and she finds fulfillment in her new career.

Solution creators have fired the paradigm gatekeeper stationed in the guardhouse between their ears—and in the minds of others. When faced with a situation in need of a solution, the average person will run through the mental rolodex of standard or acceptable fixes. These standards are based upon the expectations of others and upon the performance mentality developed through the internalization of those expectations. Therefore the average person self-censors outside-the-box solutions for fear of being rejected. Worse, they often heap layers of self-rejection upon themselves.

Solution creators do not stand on ceremony or preoccupy themselves with the preservation of obsolete paradigms. They are committed to resisting and overcoming the fear of change, and they refuse to be blinded or blindsided by it. Solution creators don't worship at the altar of public opinion or cultural norms because they realize these have the character of shifting sands. Instead, solution creators look for approval from within, always with an eye on their life's purpose, dreams, and values.

Solution-creating example: A young wife is faced with a difficult question: whether or not to seek marital counseling to address her husband's addiction to pornography. Her spouse denies that he is suffering from an addiction even though he is becoming increasingly obsessed and spends endless hours on the Internet.

The wife's parents and in-laws feel strongly that this matter is too personal to be shared or resolved outside the home. However, the issue is proving deleterious to the couple's physical and emotional relationship. They are spending less and less time with one another, are finding communication increasingly difficult, and are dealing with deepening trust issues stemming from the husband's need to cover his tracks.

The wife has never felt comfortable with confrontation, particularly in her marital relationship, and she knows that others will disapprove of such a transparent approach. Yet she is unwilling to see her husband and her marriage destroyed. She loves him and hopes to start a family with him.

She begins to research the subject of pornography addiction and begins to share some of what she is learning with her husband. At times he resents the intrusion, but she gently persists. She also attends a support group for women in her situation.

She shows her husband a great deal of compassion and continues to love him unconditionally. In time he is ready to admit that he has a problem. Soon after they enter counseling despite the protestations of her parents and in-laws.

As a result of her patient endurance and proactive involvement, the couple enters a season of renewed emotional intimacy. In time, they overcome the pornography challenge and are ready to start their family.

Solution-Creation Checklist

Become familiar with the five traits of solution creators described. Then apply one or more of those traits to create specific solutions for your two most pressing problems. Ask yourself the following questions where applicable and write your answers as part of the development of your solutions:

1. What new possibilities (circumstances, opportunities, paradigms) can be uncovered as a result of these problems?

2. How can I embrace the difficult moments related to these problems to create something new and beneficial out of a negative circumstance?

3. In what ways might these problems be connected to unfinished business and how can dealing with the problems free me from old limitations?

4. Am I hoping that someone will make my problems go away? If so, how can I use these challenging situations to discover my innate resourcefulness?

5. Am I allowing paradigm gatekeepers to prevent me from creating solutions to these problems? If so, what or who are they?

Your Dream Is a One-of-a-Kind Solution

Because your strategic life plan is written with your authentic dream in mind, it is a document of solutions. Why? Because your dream is a solution to something...for somebody...somewhere.

History bears witness to the power of a single dream and a solitary dreamer. Jonas Salk, the developer of the polio vaccine, was a man with a big dream: He was determined to create a solution for polio. He knew his dream had the potential to profoundly impact the world because he was familiar with the devastation the disease had inflicted over the centuries.

Salk became intrigued with the study of viruses while he was still in medical school, and he pursued this field of study for years. Here is part of his amazing life story, as told in the *American Academy of Achievement* Website article entitled, "The Calling to Find a Cure":

> While attending medical school at New York University, Salk was invited to spend a year researching influenza. The virus that causes flu had only recently been discovered and the young Salk was eager to learn if the virus could be deprived of its ability to infect, while still giving immunity to the

illness. Salk succeeded in this attempt, which became the basis of his later work on polio. . . . In 1955 Salk's years of research paid off. Human trials of the polio vaccine effectively protected the subject from the polio virus."[9]

The discovery of a polio vaccine was a solution of previously unimaginable magnitude. Prior to the vaccine's development and availability, parents lived with the constant fear that their children would be struck by the debilitating disease. Children and adults who contracted the disease were subject to permanent paralysis.

The world braced for regular polio epidemics and endured many outbreaks especially in the summertime. The medical community was helpless to control the spread of the highly infectious disease. Polio was a problem that seemed impossible to solve.

To create a solution, Jonas Salk stepped outside the box. Attempts to solve the problem of polio exposure had proven woefully inadequate. Salk set his sights higher. He sought to disrupt the status quo altogether by rendering the exposure harmless—his vaccine succeeded in doing so.

"Man's mind, once stretched by a new idea, never regains its original dimensions."—Oliver Wendell Holmes[10]

Except in rare cases, children growing up in the developed areas of today's world are unfamiliar with polio. Their parents are not fearful of it, their friends don't contract the disease, and they don't hear about it in the media. What a radical paradigm shift from the early 1950s when polio was on everybody's mind!

This shift happened because Jonas Salk's dream was destined to be a solution. Your dream is too! You were born to live strategically and you are reading this book because you are determined to do so. Like Jonas Salk, you were designed to plunder problems by embracing the role of solution creator.

You are a walking, breathing solution to something, and when it comes to the manner in which you handle life's problems, rest assured that you fall into one of two categories: You are either a full-blown, problem-plundering solution creator . . . or you are in the process of becoming one!

14

LIVE YOUR DREAM-POWERED, STRATEGIC LIFE

"In the winter of 1964, Nelson Mandela arrived on Robben Island where he would spend 18 of his 27 prison years. Confined to a small cell, the floor his bed, a bucket for a toilet, he was forced to do hard labor in a quarry. He was allowed one visitor a year for 30 minutes. He could write and receive one letter every six months. But Robben Island became the crucible which transformed him. Through his intelligence, charm and dignified defiance, Mandela eventually bent even the most brutal prison officials to his will, assumed leadership over his jailed comrades and became the master of his own prison. He emerged from it the mature leader who would fight and win the great political battles that would create a new democratic South Africa."[1]

Twenty-seven grueling years in prison did not break Nelson Mandela. Instead, his hardship molded him into a man fully equipped to fulfill his purpose and achieve his destiny. Like Joseph whose life we studied earlier, Mandela endured abandonment, accusation, and degradation before rising to an unprecedented position of leadership and influence on the world scene.

Against all odds Nelson Mandela emerged from the ashes of apartheid to become the first democratically elected president of South Africa—at the age of 75! Despite his years of isolation in prison, he remained attuned to his destiny code. As long hours, days, and decades ticked by, he knew that as long as the game clock was still running, there was hope of accomplishing his mission.

Nelson Mandela had uncorked his dream to end apartheid early in life. He pursued it passionately, if not perfectly, and adjusted his tactics as time wore on. While seemingly powerless in the custody of a government diametrically opposed to his mission, he nevertheless moved steadily into the realm of probability and lived to see the culmination of his greatest desire.

You too are poised on the continuum leading to your fulfilled purpose. Your dream may already be carefully framed in your heart. If not, it is percolating just beneath your emotional skin, where it is ready to erupt in a flow of words and images that will forecast your future and guide your destiny path... until the clock stops running and the scoreboard reads *Game Over*.

Full Engagement—Five Rules of the Road to Destiny

Taking up round-the-clock residency in your dream-powered, strategic life requires full engagement with the content of your life space. To live the biggest life—the one you dream of—you'll want to actively synthesize the elements of destiny pursuit you have discovered and developed so far, including:

- *The existence, meaning, and operation of your destiny code.*

- *Your knowledge of self as developed via your strategic life inventory and other exercises, introspections, and life experiences.*

- *The aspects of your dream including your mission, values, strategies, tactics, well-formed outcomes (including all goals and objectives) comprising your strategic life plan.*

- *Your understanding of seasons, elevated perspective, enthusiasm, motivation, commitment, and opportunity.*

- *The actions you choose to take based on the elements listed above.*

When these components are working together, they produce an effervescent, yet beautifully balanced blend of the theoretical and the practical. This is what powers the lives of those who live strategically. On a functional level, it will convert your powerful want-to, into a key-turning how-to and will keep the ball rolling until (and even after) the door to your chance-to flies open. (See Chapter 6.)

Below is a punch list of big-picture, proactive steps that will help keep the blend balanced as you proceed day by day and season by season toward the fulfillment of your destiny. Included are action steps for each technique.

1. *Rely on the vision of your fulfilled destiny to motivate you from within.* Genuine motivation will always be an inside job that springs, not from external sources, but from your desire to achieve your mission. It is the renewable resource that is continually refreshed by your focus on the purpose for which you were created.

   When motivation seems lacking (don't panic—it will dip at times!), first pause and then take time to reconnect with the pursuit that consistently causes you to feel fully alive. Make a careful search of your heart and circumstances to check your path. Come to grips with any unintended departures from purpose whether they were caused by a life crisis, misunderstanding, or any other form of distraction. This self-examination will help you reestablish your steps and find renewed motivation.

 ACTION STEP: BE PROACTIVE IN THE MAINTENANCE OF YOUR MOTIVATION RESERVOIR. CHECK YOUR LEVELS DAILY. THE SOONER YOU DETECT A DIP IN YOUR WANT-TO OR IDENTIFY ANY DEPLETION PATTERNS THAT IMPAIR YOUR MOTIVATION RESERVES, THE MORE APT YOU WILL BE TO IDENTIFY AND ADDRESS THE PROBLEM, RESTORE YOUR MOMENTUM, AND RETURN TO FULL ENGAGEMENT.

2. *Keep your attitudes, speech, and actions positive.* This is easier to do when your source of motivation is pure and your want-to is amply supplied. Yet even under the best of circumstances, negative tendencies can creep in and undermine your efforts.

   Establish a "court" of accountability to help you maintain a positive emotional and practical approach to your dream. Examine your own actions and invite a trustworthy mentor to hold you accountable as well. Once you are made aware, be willing to check any self-defeating attitudes at the door. Arrest habitual word choices that are not fully aligned with your stated purpose such as:

> *I hate meetings.*
> *I can't do this.*
> *We'll never get this order.*

Avoid blame-game dialect that reveals an unwillingness to take responsibility. Monitor your verbalization of blame as captured in accusatory statements such as:

> *This would have worked if only so and so would've been more supportive.*
> *They would have respected my ideas if I had gone to an Ivy League university.*

Instead, take ownership of your life. Resist fear-driven statements that undermine your belief in your self-worth and your destiny (*I'm not smart/skinny/articulate enough. My dream is more of a pipe dream than it is a worthy pursuit.*).

Be vigilant in your formation of goals; remember that pleasure-oriented goals are more effective motivators than are fear-based goals. (See Chapter 9.) Reevaluate your goals at regular intervals and be willing to adjust them as needed to produce the outcomes you desire with as few unwanted surprises as possible.

 ACTION STEP: LISTEN TO YOUR WORDS. LEARN TO HEAR YOURSELF AS AN OBJECTIVE LISTENER WOULD. SEEK TO KNOW WHETHER YOUR APPROACH TO SITUATIONS AND TO LIFE IN GENERAL IS POSITIVE OR NEGATIVE. FEEDBACK IS EVERYWHERE; BECOME COGNIZANT OF THE EFFECT OF YOUR WORDS AND ACTIONS UPON OTHERS AND UPON YOUR OWN OUTCOMES. MAKE ADJUSTMENTS AS NEEDED.

3. *Maintain a clear vision of your future, in good times and in not-so-good times.* Your dream is a powerfully motivating snapshot of your future.

Keep it in focus, even when you feel as though it is slipping away and out of reach. Rehearse your mission statement daily; reread your strategic life plan often.

Daily enter into a full sensory experience of your dream or of particular elements of your dream. Picture yourself living the life you were born to live; remind yourself of how it will feel . . . smell . . . look. Exploit the power of your God-given imagination to experience in the present what is yet to be fully manifested in your life. Use your intellectual capacities to keep the vision accurate and perfectly aligned with your authentic purpose.

 ACTION STEP: KEEP REMINDERS HANDY—PUT AN INSPIRATIONAL PHOTO OR DRAWING ON YOUR REFRIGERATOR; POST A VERBAL CONFIRMATION OF YOUR DREAM ON THE BATHROOM MIRROR (A SAYING, A JOB TITLE, *SOMETHING* THAT TRIGGERS YOUR DREAM MACHINE). DESCRIBE YOUR FUTURE TO YOUR MATE OR TO A TRUSTED MENTOR. MAKE A VOICE RECORDING THAT DESCRIBES YOUR FUTURE IN YOUR OWN WORDS AND REPLAY THE RECORDING FROM TIME TO TIME.

4. *Recognize the milestones en route to your dream.* As you run along the path that leads to the fully manifested vision for your life, take note of the landmarks along the way. Maintain a clear sense of where you came from, where you are, and where you are heading. Take ownership of your journey by being fully aware of the milestones that indicate your progress.

Embrace your accomplishments and value their meaning; take satisfaction from them and recognize their value as confidence boosters. They are representative of the reality of your dream *and* they affirm your ability to achieve it. Be clear as to which benchmarks are yet to be met and make any needed adjustments as you approach them, knowing that you are fully qualified to complete your course.

 ACTION STEP: KEEP A SCRAPBOOK OR JOURNAL SPECI-FICALLY DEDICATED TO THE DOCUMENTATION OF MILESTONE ACHIEVEMENTS. BE AS CREATIVE OR AS PRACTICAL IN YOUR

COMPILATION AS YOU LIKE. DEPENDING UPON YOUR PERSONALITY, ANYTHING FROM A FULL-BLOWN PICTORIAL TO A LIST OF BRIEF BULLET POINTS WILL DO. CHOOSE WHICHEVER METHOD YOU FIND MOST INSPIRING. YOU CAN ALSO DOCUMENT YOUR VISION OF THE MILESTONES THAT ARE YET TO BE REACHED.

5. *Assign a high priority to vision-oriented activities.* To achieve your dream, you will need to remind yourself of your priorities daily. Allow your goals to dictate the content of your consciousness so that your sense of priority will always be refreshed and aligned with your purpose. Avoid developing affection for pursuits that are outside of your plan; don't allow these distractions to sidetrack you.

Evaluate the outflow of your activities on a daily, weekly, and yearly basis. Ascertain whether the sum total of your efforts is adding up to destiny achievement. If not, stop and reevaluate your priorities; ask yourself why certain activities are not productive and redirect your energy and resources toward activities that are more likely to produce your desired outcomes. Be willing to adjust your priorities as your needs change. (Bear in mind that your strategic life plan is a document of solutions and, as such, should be considered eligible for revision or improvement in response to changing realities.)

ACTION STEP: USE VISUAL REMINDERS OF YOUR MOST PRESSING GOALS AT ANY POINT IN TIME. MARK A WHITEBOARD OR AN INDEX CARD WITH A SIMPLE PHRASE THAT DESCRIBES THE GOAL OR GOALS IN THREE OR FOUR WORDS. KEEP A DAILY TO-DO LIST TO HELP YOU STAY ON TRACK. WHEN YOU WRITE DOWN YOUR DAILY PRIORITIES, YOU INCREASE THE LIKELIHOOD THAT YOU WILL TAKE ACTION AND COMPLETE YOUR TASKS IN A TIMELY MANNER.

These big-picture pointers will help you corral your energies and enhance your efforts for maximum impact to ensure your continued progress in the direction of your dream. Next we'll explore organizational approaches that will solidify your game plan.

Organize Your Life for Success

Being organized for success means that you have in place structures and procedures to accommodate and promote the pursuit of your vision and eliminate unnecessary confusion.

Once again your strategic life plan is your primary source. Your mission statement will guide your development of organizing principles designed to help you make smart choices in the following key areas:

Career choices. Among the opportunities you will encounter are those related to career path and development. These may include choices pertaining to job placement and advancement; considerations regarding self-employment, partnerships, and career associations; chosen areas of specialty and influence; and opportunities to relocate or expand your operations.

Your strategic life plan in general and your mission statement in particular provide explicit and inferred guidance in these areas. Avoid career choices that conflict with the fundamentals of your vision, values, and purpose. At the same time take care not to dismiss a career opportunity until you have looked beneath the surface and explored any hidden advantages.

Personal and professional development activities. Honestly assess your strategic life inventory in the context of your professed life purpose. Avail yourself of any appropriate venues in which to develop your personal and professional skills and abilities. Identify areas of weakness that would benefit from additional training, education, or experience. Avoid forays into education and training that are based in questionable motives, such as the desire for titles, credentials, or other status symbols used to satisfy unmet needs for affirmation.

Your daily work schedule. Design a daily work schedule that is in tune with your mission, giftings, and circumstances. If your dream is to paint landscapes, you'll need to build your schedule around the availability of daylight. If you are a self-employed writer whose best work is achieved in the morning hours, you'll want to avoid indulging night-owl tendencies.

You will also benefit from establishing productivity targets (daily, weekly, or monthly quotas that are applicable to your work). These will help ensure a steady work flow while avoiding excessive overtime or weekend work that could prove detrimental to your health or family life. For instance, if your work is dependent upon prospecting, establish a set number of cold calls to be made each day. If you are an aspiring actor, establish a goal for the number of auditions you will schedule each month.

Growth areas. Identify the areas in which you desire to develop increased strength or capacity. Focus on growth areas that will improve character, enhance productivity, and increase endurance as it relates to the pursuit of your dream. We've already addressed the practical development of your skills and abilities. The growth areas under discussion here exist in the realms of the emotions, the spiritual life, and physical well-being.

Perhaps you are a gifted, well-trained dancer whose dream it is to be in a long-running Broadway show. If so, you know that unless you are physically, emotionally, and even spiritually prepared for the rigors of a Broadway schedule, you will not be able to achieve your dream, regardless of the excellence of your professional ability. Seek to develop these non-technical growth areas to the point that they match the intensity of your skills and will help sustain your overall efforts.

Teamwork. Whether or not your dream involves the formation of a formal team solely dedicated to the achievement of your purpose, it will involve consistent interaction with others whose participation contributes to your outcomes. This team includes, but is not limited to, outside organizations, vendors, accountants, advisors, and family members.

Whatever the composition of your team, you will involve in your pursuit those who can do for you what you cannot do for yourself. They will either accomplish tasks for which you are not well-suited or those to which you cannot wisely dedicate adequate time.

Always communicate clearly with your team so that each participant understands their specific role and your specific expectations of them. Share your purpose and provide clarity as to the elements of your game plan which involve them or are affected by their work. Help them succeed by providing clear instruction, encouragement, and feedback. Your investment in their performance is worthwhile because their success improves the quality of their lives *and* directly impacts your outcomes.

Organization in these five essential areas will improve the quality of your life experience and enhance your results by streamlining your career track; maximizing your abilities and attributes; improving productivity, minimizing procrastination, and avoiding time-wasters; reducing clutter (including emotional clutter), increasing your endurance, and promoting overall well-being.

Perhaps most importantly, being organized for success will equip you to stand against the threats that travel hand in hand with opportunity. Organization will help you take opposition and obstacles in stride and will enable you to use challenges as stepping stones to your dream.

Discover Your Mentor

One of the key members of your team is someone who may not be immediately evident to you and may not hail from your inner circle. Yet this person is uniquely equipped to perceive your potential, affirm your calling, and walk with you from the hallway of the unknown to the terra firma of your fully-developed dream.

That key member is a mentor, a formidable and trustworthy person who understands what it will take for you to succeed in destiny fulfillment. Your mentor recognizes the yearnings that proceed from the depths of your destiny code and knows how to unleash their power.

The right mentor has the uncanny ability to hear your heart almost as if it were his or her own. Your mentor is willing to be a sounding board, a safe place for you to utter your destiny-related desires without being made vulnerable to ridicule or self-rejection. This is someone you can count on to be frank without shutting you down—a person big enough to engage in a transparent, productive relationship that does not revolve around their needs, but rather exists to promote your success.

The mentoring relationship involves the uncommon level of emotional intimacy that is able to support growth and maturation. A good mentor will not coddle you. Instead your mentor will draw you out of your comfort zone and hold you accountable for measurable progress en route to your dream.

A diligent mentor will expose attempts at excuse-making and will help you uncover and dispel any unspoken fears or self-limiting attitudes and behaviors. In so doing, your mentor will foster genuine healing and make room for you to be authentic, both personally and professionally.

Your mentor's incisive input will also promote clarity of mind and purpose; it will hone your ability to make crucial decisions and inspire the very choices that can unlock your potential and counter the din of distraction.

Mentoring also provides an invisible pipeline of supply. Your mentor can connect you with people and resources to which you wouldn't otherwise have access. Your mentor is a depository of knowledge and experience. He or she has gone before you and has already blazed useful trails through what appears to be uncharted territory. The knowledge your mentor offers is more than head knowledge; it includes an intuitive grasp of your uniqueness, including an understanding of its value and the capacity to inspire its development.

Your mentor is able to read your destiny code and is drawn to you by what it reveals. Your mentor is positioned to awaken within you a greater awareness of your potential and will help you recognize the depths of your capacity—both to achieve and to influence others.

To benefit from your involvement with a mentor and to keep the mentoring relationship thriving, you must *desire* what the mentor has to offer. At the most fundamental level, your mentoring relationship is based on your desire to learn. Any teacher can tell you that...

- *One of the greatest keys to learning is hunger.*
- *One of the primary triggers to hunger is desire.*
- *And one of the most potent precursors to desire is attraction.*

Your desire to learn from a mentoring relationship rests largely in your attraction to what the mentor knows and is able to model for you. But this relationship must be reciprocal: Your mentor will be attracted by the opportunity to awaken the elements revealed in your destiny code and will look for signs that...

You also long for this awakening.

You have decided that you must experience it (and the destiny it foretells).

You want to have and do whatever is necessary to live your dream.

Often the mentoring relationship will lead you into a season of necessary discomfort. This occurs when your mentor ignites in you the desire for what he or she has modeled. This in turn triggers your dissatisfaction with the sense of constriction imposed by residual inside-the-box tendencies.

Once you glimpse the freedom your mentor has defined by example, you will be unable to comfortably climb back into an old paradigm. And if you attempt to retreat to safety, your mentor will call you to account and urge you to embrace the opportunity to redefine yourself and abolish the status quo.

Your mentor understands and will never let you forget that you were created for greatness. How could you forget, really? You are one of a kind. No one—absolutely no one!—compares to you. Your dream has been uncorked and its power has been activated. The world is waiting to feel its impact, waiting for the solution that does not yet exist in its collective memory—the very solution that was written into your destiny code before your name was heard.

Your destiny awaits; it will be fulfilled by you or not at all. It will be enjoyed by you or by no one. It will speak to the miracle of your creation and will fulfill your every desire. While there is still breath in your lungs *you, and only you, can live your dream.*

The keys are in your hand.

The place is set.

The time is *now.*

ENDNOTES

Chapter 1: Uncork Your Dream

1. http://www.quotationspage.com/quotes/Victor_Hugo/ (accessed December 10, 2007).

Chapter 2: Decode Your Destiny

1. http://www.quotationspage.com/quotes/Georgia O%27Keeffe/ (accessed December 19, 2007).

2. http://www.ellafitzgerald.com/index.php?option=com_content& task=view&id=12&Itemid=28 (accessed December 19, 2007).

3. http://www.annefrank.org/content.asp?pid=122&lid=2 (accessed December 20, 2007).

Chapter 3: Take Your Strategic Life Inventory

1. http://pawprints.kashalinka.com/anecdotes/aquinas.shtml (accessed December 29, 2007).

2. values. Dictionary.com. *The American Heritage® Dictionary of the English Language, Fourth Edition.* Houghton Mifflin Company, 2004. http:// dictionary.reference.com/browse/values (accessed January 1, 2008).

Chapter 4: Embrace the Seasons of Your Life

1. http://www.digitaldreamdoor.com/pages/music_rm/turn_turn_ turn.html (accessed January 4, 2008).

2. http://pawprints.kashalinka.com/anecdotes/shaw.shtml (accessed January 5, 2008).

3. http://pawprints.kashalinka.com/anecdotes/barton.shtml (accessed January 5, 2008).

4. burr. Dictionary.com. *The American Heritage® Dictionary of the English Language, Fourth Edition*. Houghton Mifflin Company, 2004. http://dictionary.reference.com/browse/burr (accessed: January 09, 2008).

5. http://www.bartleby.com/66/68/39068.html (accessed January 6, 2008).

6. http://www.bartleby.com/66/58/14258.html (accessed January 6, 2008).

Chapter 5: Check Out Your Outcomes

1. http://www.quotationspage.com/quotes/Robert_Burns/ (accessed January 14, 2008).

2. http://www.baseball-almanac.com/quotes/quorose.shtml (accessed January 14, 2008).

3. http://pawprints.kashalinka.com/anecdotes/aaron.shtml (accessed January 14, 2008).

4. http://www.bartleby.com/63/3/8603.html (accessed January 15, 2008).

5. gap. Dictionary.com. *The American Heritage® Dictionary of the English Language, Fourth Edition*. Houghton Mifflin Company, 2004. http://dictionary.reference.com/browse/gap (accessed January 15, 2008).

6. http://pawprints.kashalinka.com/anecdotes/williams_tennessee.shtml (accessed January 14, 2008).

7. http://pawprints.kashalinka.com/anecdotes/bernhardt.shtml (accessed January 14, 2008).

Chapter 6: Build Your Life on Higher Ground

1. http://www.quoteworld.org/quotes/2918 (accessed January 19, 2008).

2. blueprint. Dictionary.com. *Dictionary.com Unabridged (v 1.1)*. Random House, Inc. http://dictionary.reference.com/browse/blueprint (accessed: January 20, 2008).

3. http://www.brainyquote.com/quotes/authors/f/frank_lloyd_wright.html (accessed January 20, 2008).

4. http://www.brainyquote.com/quotes/authors/w/w_clement_stone.html (accessed February 27, 2008).

5. Joseph Jaworski, "Destiny and the Leader," http://www.generonconsulting.com/publications/papers/pdfs/Destiny%20and%20the%20Leader.pdf (accessed January 28, 2008).

6. John C. Maxwell, *The Difference Maker* (Nashville: Thomas Nelson, 2006).

Chapter 7: Think Outside the Box

1. http://www.designboom.com/eng/interview/libeskind.html (accessed January 21, 2008).

2. http://news-service.stanford.edu/news/2005/june15/jobs-061505.html (accessed January 22, 2008).

3. dogma. Dictionary.com. *Dictionary.com Unabridged (v 1.1)*. Random House, Inc. http://dictionary.reference.com/browse/dogma (accessed: January 22, 2008).

4. http://news-service.stanford.edu/news/2005/june15/jobs-061505.html (accessed January 22, 2008).

5. http://www.quotationspage.com/subjects/computers/ (accessed January 22, 2008).

Chapter 8: Commit Your Strategic Life Plan to Paper

1. http://www.brainyquote.com/quotes/authors/v/victor_hugo.html (accessed January 28, 2008).

2. Joseph Jaworski, "Destiny and the Leader," http://www.generonconsulting.com/publications/papers/pdfs/Destiny%20and%20the%20Leader.pdf (accessed January 28, 2008).

3. http://hanover.redcross.org/mission.htm (accessed January 29, 2008).

4. http://pawprints.kashalinka.com/anecdotes/wordsworth.shtml (accessed January 29, 2008).

5. feasibility. Dictionary.com. *The American Heritage® Dictionary of the English Language, Fourth Edition.* Houghton Mifflin Company, 2004. http://dictionary.reference.com/browse/feasibility (accessed January 29, 2008).

6. cost. Dictionary.com. *The American Heritage® Dictionary of the English Language, Fourth Edition.* Houghton Mifflin Company, 2004. http://dictionary.reference.com/browse/cost (accessed January 29, 2008).

7. function. Dictionary.com. *The American Heritage® Dictionary of the English Language, Fourth Edition.* Houghton Mifflin Company, 2004. http://dictionary.reference.com/browse/function (accessed January 29, 2008).

8. American Cancer Society, "Image 5 pdf."

Chapter 9: Unleash the Power of Your Goals

1. http://www.quotationspage.com/quote/2595.html (accessed January 31, 2008).

2. benchmark. Dictionary.com. *The American Heritage® Dictionary of the English Language, Fourth Edition.* Houghton Mifflin Company, 2004. http://dictionary.reference.com/browse/benchmark (accessed February 1, 2008).

3. enthusiasm. Dictionary.com. *The American Heritage® Dictionary of the English Language, Fourth Edition.* Houghton Mifflin Company, 2004. http://dictionary.reference.com/browse/enthusiasm (accessed February 1, 2008).

4. http://pawprints.kashalinka.com/anecdotes/wright_bros.shtml (accessed February 1, 2008).

5. http://www.quotationspage.com/quotes/Ralph_Waldo_Emerson/31 (accessed February 1, 2008).

6. http://www.quoteworld.org/quotes/7159 (accessed February 1, 2008).

7. 1 Timothy 6:10 (The New American Standard Bible Update).

Chapter 10: Face Down Fear

1. John Maxwell, *The Difference Maker* (Nashville: Thomas Nelson, 2006).

2. http://www.quotationspage.com/quote/27730.html (accessed February 2, 2008).

3. fatalism. Dictionary.com. *Dictionary.com Unabridged (v 1.1)*. Random House, Inc. http://dictionary.reference.com/browse/fatalism (accessed February 8, 2008).

4. Joseph Jaworski, "Destiny and the Leader," http://www.generonconsulting.com/publications/papers/pdfs/Destiny%20and%20the%20Leader.pdf (accessed January 28, 2008).

5. John Ortberg, *If You Want to Walk on Water, You've Got to Get Out of the Boat* (Grand Rapids: Zondervan, 2001).

Chapter 11: Tap Into Opportunity

1. http://www.quotationspage.com/quote/29680.html (accessed February 13, 2008).

2. http://pawprints.kashalinka.com/jokes/index.html?http&&&pawprints.ka shalinka.com/jokes/used_cars.shtml.

3. http://www.quotationspage.com/quote/1722.html.

4. Mark J. Chironna, *You Can Let Go Now* (Nashville: Thomas Nelson, 2004).

Chapter 12: Transform Possibility Into Probability

1. http://pawprints.kashalinka.com/anecdotes/perot.shtml (accessed February 19, 2008).

2. http://www.quotationspage.com/quotes/Thomas_A._Edison/ (accessed February 21, 2008).

3. possibility. Dictionary.com. *WordNet®* *3.0*. Princeton University. http://dictionary.reference.com/browse/possibility (accessed February 20, 2008).

4. probability. Dictionary.com. *WordNet®* *3.0*. Princeton University. http://dictionary.reference.com/browse/probabily (accessed February 20, 2008).

5. reality. Dictionary.com. *WordNet®* *3.0*. Princeton University. http://dictionary.reference.com/browse/reality (accessed February 20, 2008).

Chapter 13: Stop Solving Problems and Start Creating Solutions

1. http://www.quotationspage.com/subjects/creativity/ (accessed February 21, 2008).

2. http://www.georgelois.com/bio.html (accessed February 22, 2008).

3. http://www.quotationspage.com/subjects/imagination/ (accessed February 22, 2008).

4. http://www.quotationspage.com/subjects/imagination/ (accessed February 21, 2008). http://www.quotationspage.com/subjects/ideas/ (accessed February 22, 2008).

5. Michael Wolff, "Candidate.com," *New York Magazine*, September 15, 2003, http://nymag.com/nymetro/news/media/columns/medialife/n_9188/ (accessed February 23, 2008).

6. Ibid.

7. http://www.quotationspage.com/subjects/creativity/ (accessed February 21, 2008).

8. http://www.quotationspage.com/quotes/Thomas_A._Edison/ (accessed February 21, 2008).

9. Academy of Achievement, "The Calling to Find a Cure," http://www.achievement.org/autodoc/page/sal0bio-1 (accessed February 23, 2008).

10. http://www.quotationspage.com/subjects/ideas/ (accessed February 22, 2008).

Chapter 14: Live Your Dream-Powered, Strategic Life

1. PBS *Frontline*, "The Prisoner," http://www.pbs.org/wgbh/pages/frontline/shows/mandela/prison/ (accessed February 26, 2008).

4-WEEK

STUDY
GUIDE

TABLE OF CONTENTS

Week 4

UNCORK YOUR DREAM

"Whatever your circumstances and past experiences, there is infinite promise still ahead. Your dreams may be covered in dust; they may even be shattered into tiny pieces, but deep down you know the game clock is still running. Something inside you is saying, *As long as there is breath in my lungs, my dreams can come true.*"

Discover Your Dream

- Do you have a dream? Maybe you've never even thought of dreaming a dream because your life has always been just a series of reactions to life's circumstances. Plan to take some quiet time alone and think about the things that make you smile, memories that make your heart flutter, times when you thought, *Gee, that is something I'd love to try!*

- Thinking about the sports team analogy in Chapter 1, has there been a time when you were involved in an activity and it just "felt right"? Or you saw someone on television or at work and you could "see yourself" doing the same thing—even better?

- Enjoy imagining all the possible possibilities and write down anything and everything that comes to mind.

Define Your Dream

After discovering—or rediscovering—your dream, it needs to be defined. Rather than having a pie-in-the-sky type of dream that is just nice to think about once in awhile, defining your dream will give it substance which will set in motion the actions to make it come true. Complete the following sentences:

My dream is

_____

_____

_____

My dream will

_____

_____

_____

My dream can

_____

_____

_____

My dream helps

_____

_____

_____

My dream can be achieved by

_____

_____

_____

My dream will come true when I

_____

_____

_____

Declare Your Dream

Sharing your dream with your spouse or close friend will give you confidence to pursue it. Make sure the person you confide in is one who will be encouraging and inspiring. Of course your very best friend, God, is always present, encouraging, and inspiring and would love to be part of making your heart's desires come true.

Develop Your Dream

"Strategic planners live intentionally." What does this statement mean to you?

_____

_____

_____

"Your life is not an accident, regardless of the circumstances surrounding your conception. When you recognize and embrace this fundamental truth, you are empowered to become a more active participant in the formation of your future. Instead of wondering how your life will turn out, *you become the architect of your destiny; you draw the plans, and you live the dream.*" What can you do today to start building your dream?

_____

_____

_____

Dedicate Your Dream

Ensuring that God is smack dab in the middle of your planning will make all the difference. Take time each day to listen for His voice directing you along the way.

Remember: "Faith in your dream, when combined with curiosity and imagination, can bring elements of the future into your present reality."

DECODE YOUR DESTINY

"Your destiny code is one of a kind. It is the system of symbols, signals, and patterns that you experience both in your thoughts and throughout your external circumstances. Included in your destiny code are your relationships and the providential connections that pave the way to your dreams. Your destiny code is woven into your life's fabric and is reflected in the unique events which you have experienced. When you become aware of it, your destiny code will reveal your unique identity, purpose, and path. It is a detailed picture of your potential."

Discover Your Dream

When reading the stories about Joseph, Ella Fitzgerald, Kate, Anne Frank, and Frank Sinatra, could you relate to any aspects of their lives? Did parts of their stories "ring true" within?

- "Hints to your destiny code are often found in your relationships." Think about your spouse, significant other, and close friends. Have they said something similar about you over the years that may form a pattern? Examples can range from: people coming to you with their problems to hear your wise advice to people asking you to style their hair because it comes so naturally to you.

- "Your destiny code can also be revealed in the things you love to do." Do you like to work with your hands? Sing? Play sports? Volunteer at fairs, hospitals, or schools? Do you like to plant flowers? Hammer nails?

Coach midget football? Think about all the things that you really like to do, and then narrow that list down to one special thing that you are really good at.

- "Destiny codes can be revealed in the *way* you do things." You may have a certain "pizzazz" or "flair" when doing something. From organizing a bake sale to your home's curb appeal to setting a beautiful table, think about the things that people have complimented you about . . . and then take that thing and use it as another key to decode your destiny.

Define Your Dream

List three things that could have kept Joseph from reaching his full potential:

1.

2.

3.

List three things that put Joseph in the right place at the right time to fulfill his potential:

1.

2.

3.

List three things that could have kept Ella Fitzgerald from reaching her full potential:

1.

2.

3.

List three things that put Ella Fitzgerald in the right place at the right time to fulfill her potential:

1.

2.

3.

List three things that could keep you from reaching your full potential:

1.

2.

3.

List three things that put you in the right place at the right time to fulfill your potential:

1.

2.

3.

Explain your personal lists in more detail:

_____

_____

_____

Declare Your Dream

"Your Authentic Identity: This is your true self, the 'real you' free of all masks, cover-ups, and false projections. Your authentic identity reveals your God-given uniqueness and underpins your God-given destiny." Write what you believe is the "real you"—be nice to yourself and include personality traits; ambitions; and mental, spiritual, and physical attributes of the "ideal you."

_____

_____

_____

Develop Your Dream

"Your destiny code reveals your inner workings; it shows just what makes you tick *and why*." How much of yourself is a result of "nature" or "nurture"? Do you think your parents, siblings, and environment had more influence over the way you are now, or do you think you have had more control over the type of person you are now? Write about what you think "makes you tick and why."

_____

_____

_____

Dedicate Your Dream

Allowing God to walk with you daily as you live your dream and fulfill your destiny assures you of the most rewarding and best outcome imaginable. When tough times or challenges arise, He will be there to remind you of the "big picture."

Remember: "Regardless of the field of endeavor, each potential innovator (you!) comes to understand the value of his or her unique factor and realizes that it may be the very answer for which the world (your family, your workplace, your church, your community) is waiting."

TAKE YOUR STRATEGIC LIFE INVENTORY

"When you don't know what is inside of you—the dreams...abilities...even the unique way you are wired for a specific kind of success—you cannot and will not grasp the loss that would be suffered by letting it go to waste."

Discover Your Dream

- "A dream pursued always affects your lifestyle." If you are pursuing your dream, how has your lifestyle changed since you began your quest? If you haven't started on your journey yet, how do you think your lifestyle will change? Are you (honestly) looking forward to the change?

- "When you focus on your dream, your point of view and priorities become crystal clear." Sometimes it's easier to just "go along" in life as it is—why "rock the boat." But most times life's circumstances can be improved, and focusing on your dream can turn that row boat into a luxury liner ready to take you to dreamy places! Think about a perfect vacation spot—bask in the moment.

- "By nature, we prefer to seek immediate gratification, minimize sacrifice, and avoid opposition. But a dream can help us handle our emotions in more productive ways." All of us have pleasant and not-so-pleasant memories of extreme emotional upheavals ranging from sobbing at weddings to losing our temper. Keeping a dream alive within can help tone down emotions that can cause harm to ourselves and others. Remember a time when thinking about your dream may have changed a situation for the better.

Define Your Dream

Taking inventory of your life gives you the tools you need to stock your life with all the essentials. Review your inventory as a treat!

Has your self-confidence grown as a result of cultivating your willpower to pursue your dream in earnest?

_____

_____

_____

Has your dream redirected your emotions and improved self-control?

_____

_____

_____

Has your dream generated increased creativity? In what areas?

_____

_____

_____

Will your new ways of thinking help you rise above old obstacles and exceed previous standards? How?

_____

_____

_____

Declare Your Dream

Declaring your core criteria—*desire, intent,* and *passion*—plays an important role in fulfilling your potential and achieving your dream. Your core criteria come from within. Present your core criteria in a statement to share with your spouse or close friend. Believe what you say.

Develop Your Dream

"Your values are your deeply-held beliefs, the things you consider to be most important, and the things you are willing to live and die for." Your values shape your character and will develop your dream. List your values and write why you hold these beliefs.

_____

_____

_____

Dedicate Your Dream

God will also take inventory of your life. His desire is for you to live abundantly and to fulfill His destiny for you. Seek His guidance as you live life to its full capacity.

Remember: "Reflect on your inventory often, especially when you need to be reminded of how much you have to offer. A heightened awareness of your assets will dispel the false negatives that undermine self-image and limit life outcomes."

EMBRACE THE SEASONS OF YOUR LIFE

"Life's seasons don't always seem to fit together. Yet even at their most disorderly and perplexing, they are a hallmark of life's design, the logical way in which life's journey unfolds. They add to our lives maturity, nuance, texture, and the element of surprise. Seasons keep us agile and responsive to changing circumstances. They discourage us from setting up camp beside stagnant waters. And when we're attentive, each season reveals new vistas of opportunity."

Discover Your Dream

- "Puberty is one of life's quintessential seasons." Remember those years when you weren't "a kid" and you weren't "a grown-up"? Those were some tough times for a lot of people. Were you formulating dreams back then that you could now resurrect? Why or why not?

- "How much treasure you extract from each season has everything to do with the way in which you respond to it, whether with appreciation or disdain . . . desire or denial . . . reactivity or proactivity." How would you best describe yourself? As a person who appreciates, desires, and is proactive? Or someone who is critical, lives in denial, and reacts to situations? Are these traits prohibiting or contributing to your treasure hunt?

- "With every seasonal change in life, there are shifts in the weather, both externally (in your circumstances or relationships) and internally (in your feelings or in your changing needs and desires)." How strong is your faith during the mild and enjoyable weather? How about during the cold and stormy weather?

Define Your Dream

There are four common climate changes (internal signposts): *closed doors, relational shifts, changing needs and desires,* and *feelings of constriction.*

Have you encountered a closed door in your career? Spiritual life? Church? Marriage? What steps can you take to open other doors of opportunity that may lead you into a new career direction? Deeper walk with God? More service to others? Deeper marriage commitment?

_____

_____

_____

Have relationships at work, church, and/or socially been shifting to form new patterns? If yes, do you think you are being prepared to walk through a new door? If not, are you open to establishing new relationships? Why or why not?

_____

_____

_____

Has the excitement gone out of your daily routine? Do you feel as if you are ready to move up to another level of opportunity? How can you make this happen?

_____

_____

_____

Are you feeling frustrated and think that you are not living up to your potential? Does it seem like your skills and talents are being constricted? Write a few ways you can change your circumstances—detail your plan.

_____

_____

_____

Declare Your Dream

If you declare and are determined to take ownership of every season and deal with life's ups and downs in a positive manner, every circumstance will become an opportunity for victory. Are you taking advantage of all the opportunities that God is providing for you?

Develop Your Dream

"Your ability to advance in every type of climate is dependent upon your willingness to focus on the positives in every season." Many people remain stagnant in life because they have a negative attitude. Are you willing to move ahead with a positive attitude? What are some positives you will focus on?

_____

_____

_____

_____

Dedicate Your Dream

Thank God for all the seasons in your life. He has directed all of the climates you have encountered and has been your Protector and Encourager all along the way. Dedicate your life and dreams to Him.

Remember: "Take stock of the season you are in and get every last drop of goodness out of it. Tune into the signals that reveal the season that is ahead. You have an amazing life to live and a destiny to fulfill.

Your future is bright and wonderful and you are uniquely equipped to design it, strategically."

CHECK OUT YOUR OUTCOMES

"Outcomes are formed over time. Likewise, the improvement of outcomes is a process. It is important to appreciate this obvious but inconvenient truth: Every outcome you experience will develop over time. Therefore, if you are determined to experience better outcomes in the future, you will need to accept the fact that the changes you desire may not be achieved instantly."

Discover Your Dream

- The performance gap involves the difference between your planned performance and your actual performance. Is there a gap between what you planned to do and what you actually accomplished? Why?

_____

_____

_____

- The awareness gap occurs when you fail to take the right actions at the right time and you unwittingly put your dreams on hold. Can you think of examples of when this happened? Write how you could have been more aware, which would have moved your dreams forward.

_____

_____

_____

• The attitude gap is communicated to others either verbally or nonverbally through body language, posture, eye movements, facial expressions, and tentative behaviors. How can you improve your attitude gap today?

_____

_____

_____

Define Your Dream

"Poor planning is the perfect pathway to panic" and "those who fail to plan, plan to fail" are well-worn because they are true.

Have you developed a clear sense of precisely what you want and what you don't want? Write your thoughts here now.

_____

_____

_____

A well-formed outcome describes and defines what you want to achieve expressed in vivid, positive language that is personal and specific. Write your thoughts here now.

_____

_____

_____

A good plan includes an explanation of _why_ you want to achieve your goal. Write your thoughts here now.

_____

_____

_____

A well-formed plan considers all suitable approaches, addresses realistic timeframes, and considers whether key factors are in your control. Do you have a well-formed plan? Why or why not?

_____

_____

_____

Declare Your Dream

After writing your press release (see below), read it to your special confidant.

Develop Your Dream

Write a press release about your strategic life plan; don't forget the who, what, when, where, why, and how of your plan.

_____

_____

_____

Dedicate Your Dream

Your outcomes are only as good as your plans. Do you believe your dream is worth the time and effort it will take to devise a good plan? There is One who can give you all the assistance you need. Listen for His direction.

Remember: The future is *yours*. Only you can design it.

BUILD YOUR LIFE ON HIGHER GROUND

"Vision and the passion engendered by your vision will enable you to design your life from the inside out—from the place where your ideas originate to the physical world in which your dream becomes reality."

Discover Your Dream

- Your vision is the energizing force that stamps your present with your belief in the future. Think of your ideal future—include all the small details that will make your vision real.

- Your vision works from the inside out and sets in motion events and actions that bring your destiny to fruition. What internal changes need to be made to line up with your vision?

_____

_____

_____

- Your vision will affect your imagination and ignite your creativity. How hard will it be for you to train your brain to go in the same direction as your dream?

_____

_____

_____

Define Your Dream

To maintain an elevated (higher-ground) perspective you need to focus on bigger, more consequential ideas and thoughts that are relevant to your destiny.

An elevated perspective helps you to think big and see past obstacles and keep your eyes fixed on your vision. What obstacles are keeping you from seeing your desired end result?

_____

_____

_____

An elevated perspective prevents you from becoming entangled by the past. What issues from your past keep you from building your life on higher ground? Write them down and then cross them out on the paper and in your mind.

_____

_____

_____

The view from higher ground provides opportunities to be seized and threats to be neutralized. Write a few examples of this truth.

_____

_____

_____

An elevated perspective empowers you to give up what is *good* for what is *best*. Many people settle for what is good and comfortable. Why should you strive for the *best*?

_____

_____

_____

Declare Your Dream

"Your life light includes what others see in you and how they are affected by being in your presence." Describe your "life light" in terms that a child could understand.

_____

_____

_____

Develop Your Dream

Having a higher-ground outlook allows you to be a positive influence in every situation and opportunity. Write about a time when you took the "high road" rather than following others.

_____

_____

_____

Your gifts, talents, abilities, and other attributes do not operate in a vacuum. How have you shared yourself lately to the betterment of others?

_____

_____

_____

"Attitudes reflect perspective and drive behavior; the actions you take determine your results." Do you believe that having a bad attitude will drive you to bad behavior? Is the opposite true? Why?

_____

_____

_____

Dedicate Your Dream

Building your life on higher ground will stand for many generations if the foundation is on the rock-solid Word of God. Allow Him to build alongside you.

Remember: "You are a one-of-a-kind masterpiece equipped with a multitude of attributes designed for destiny fulfillment. You have a unique factor which sets you apart from everyone else and which is only yours to give."

THINK OUTSIDE THE BOX

"The box is nothing more than a coffin for your dreams. Inside-the-box thinking snuffs out vision and leaves in its wake the fear-clad *mis*belief that there is no way out."

Discover Your Dream

- People like to live in boxes because they are comfortable. We list the nests we make and being creatures of habit don't like to change. Is this true for you?

- Even the sounds inside our boxes are soothing. We hear what we want to hear and drown out any extraneous noises with the sound of our own voices. Is this true for you?

- All the things we think we need are in our boxes. If occasionally we need something more, we take control and maneuver just far enough to reach out, retrieve the thing, and then pull our heads back inside. Is this true for you?

Define Your Dream

"For your imagination to keep you in touch with your dream, you must follow it outside the box." What does this statement mean to you?

_____

_____

_____

What have you seen with your mind's eye but question whether it is humanly possible to achieve?

_____

_____

_____

"Outside-the-box thinking is a prerequisite for strategic living." True or false? Why?

_____

_____

_____

What are your thoughts about the Steve Jobs's story? Do you know someone who thought outside the box and succeeded? What (or who) pushed them forward?

_____

_____

_____

Declare Your Dream

Are you afraid of change? Are you in a position at work, at home, in school, at church that may be holding you back from becoming all you could become? Take a stand for your future. Reach out and speak out.

Develop Your Dream

In the story about the little girl who wanted to become a priest, it was noted that "Out of that 'created world' came a new venue and an opportunity to serve in another." How are you going about creating a place in your world that will become an exciting dream to realize?

_____

_____

_____

Dedicate Your Dream

Parents, spouse, friends, family and coworkers may try and discourage you from reaching your goals or living your dream—stay the course. Your Creator knows the beginning from the end.

Remember: If the outlet for your dream is not apparent, don't quit on your dream. If you don't have a typical job description, then carve out a place for what you do. Create demand for what you have to give by creating your own sustainable advantage—the very feature that is so distinctive as to give you a competitive and unbeatable edge.

COMMIT YOUR STRATEGIC LIFE PLAN TO PAPER

"Your strategic life plan is the blueprint for your main event and writing it down makes all the difference. You need a strategic life plan that will speak to you day in and day out, in good times and in bad...a plan that will encourage you and remind you that your dream is alive."

Discover Your Dream

Are you ready to:

- Identify your destiny code?
- Commit to your life's vision and mission?
- Write your strategic life plan?
- Proactively pursue your dream?

Define Your Dream

Re-read Chapter 8, then write your strategic life plan.

Write a clear statement of your vision. Your vision is a description of what your fulfilled destiny will look like.

_____

_____

_____

_____

Consider your mission and write a succinct short paragraph stating the purpose for which you were created, the values central to your purpose, and how you will accomplish your mission.

_____

_____

_____

Write a description of the strategies and tactics that will serve the mission, which includes your gifts, talents, and other attributes; your financial, human, and other resources including your life properties (life space, life volume, life texture, and life light); and your strengths.

_____

_____

_____

List and describe each of the goals you hope to achieve.

_____

_____

_____

Write a description of available opportunities and existing threats.

_____

_____

_____

Summarize the cost and commitment to accept the reasonable burden associated with your destiny fulfillment.

_____

_____

_____

Declare Your Dream

Commit to your plan and keep it close at hand and heart. Declare its importance in your life. Sharing your plan with another may help keep your commitment strong.

Develop Your Dream

"Consider writing a series of strategic life plans, each of which covers the key areas of your life (spiritual, social, financial, professional, family, etc.). Doing so will help you harmonize the many facets of your life into a balanced, comprehensive design." Do you think writing a series of plans will enhance your life even more? Why or why not?

_____

_____

_____

Dedicate Your Dream

Dedicating your strategic life plan to your heavenly Father will bring you peace. Acknowledging His grace and mercy in all that you do will bring you everlasting joy.

Remember: "That's where intentionality comes in. No one can expect to live their life's dream by sitting passively by and *hoping* for the right future to show up. Your strategic life plan must rest on clear, strong intent and the belief that you can and will fulfill your destiny—that you can and will make a difference."

UNLEASH THE POWER OF YOUR GOALS

"Your careful strategic planning has positioned you for *increased effectiveness* in every destiny-inspired endeavor. No longer will you cross your fingers and hope for something good to happen. Instead you will run with your vision and watch expectantly as your destiny unfurls."

Discover Your Dream

- Goal-oriented people are time and energy conscious; their lives take on the structure needed to accommodate the unfolding of their dreams.

- When your goals are in harmony with your life's calling, you are free to live out your intentions. That sense of purpose will govern your time expenditures and help you to avoid ruts and rabbit trails.

- Your well-directed choices will promote an atmosphere of order, an environment in which life's many pieces are easily fitted in place to form the big picture of your dream.

Define Your Dream

"Interaction with your goals involves discerning the quality of your activity, determining the nature of your goals, and monitoring the progress of your goals."

How do you define the *essential activities* necessary for the achievement of your goals?

_____

_____

_____

Prioritize *fulfilling activities* that give you a sense of living the "good life." How do these activities correlate with your essential activities?

_____

_____

_____

Where do *unfulfilling activities* fit into your "good life" living? How hard will they be to give up?

_____

_____

_____

Of the three goals that produce a sense of well-being—intimacy, spirituality, generativity—which one seems most beneficial to you? Why?

_____

_____

_____

Declare Your Dream

Enthusiasm is contagious. If you are enthused about achieving your goals and living your dream, others will (sometimes eventually) want to go along for the exciting ride. Think of ways you can share your enthusiasm with those in your sphere of influence.

Develop Your Dream

"The higher the level of motivation, the higher the level of commitment. . . . The higher the level of commitment, the higher the level of achievement." These statements are filled with life truth. Rewrite them in your own words.

_____

_____

_____

Dedicate Your Dream

Without goals people lose direction. Stay on the path that leads toward reaching your goals and living your dream.

Remember: "Don't keep your enthusiasm to yourself. Become a carrier of expectancy and hope for the future. Infect everyone you know and watch the tide rise around you."

WEEK 3

FACE DOWN FEAR

"Unbounded fear is the enemy of destiny. It is a cruel and illegitimate taskmaster known to exact a high price from those whom it enslaves."

Discover Your Dream

- Fear keeps you from developing and maintaining an elevated perspective. Fear promotes the sense of being weighed down and unable to cope with everyday life.

- Fear restricts you to inside-the-box thinking. Fear causes you to expect the worst and overshadows your expectation of reward.

- Fear denies you the clarity to move forward and makes you more susceptible to unforgiveness, victim mentality, pessimism, procrastination, passivity, and timidity.

Define Your Dream

Failure is a fact of life—but one that most people want to avoid. To circumvent fear, we often pave complex, costly routes around it.

How can *fatalism* kill a dream?

_____

_____

_____

Are you guilty of *task-avoidance?* Why or why not?

_____

_____

_____

Have you allowed a dream or invention to die because you didn't want to take the time or effort to experiment?

_____

_____

_____

To avoid the possibility of failure have you avoided taking an honest assessment of your outcomes?

_____

_____

_____

Declare Your Dream

"Remind yourself that success is achieved incrementally. It is not based upon a single performance. Success is based on persistence and percentages." Repeat aloud: "Success is based on persistence and percentages."

Develop Your Dream

"Everyone with a dream has a choice to make: Whether to face down the fears associated with paying the price of that dream or to risk missing the dream altogether." Prayerfully consider this choice before making your decision.

Dedicate Your Dream

I sought the Lord, and He heard me, and delivered me from all my fears (Psalm 34:4 NKJV).

Remember: "Your dream is powerful. Draw on that power to help you stay focused and lock fear out of your life. When you force your fear to look your dream in the eye, fear doesn't stand a chance of winning."

TAP INTO OPPORTUNITY

"Whether or not you are aware of them, you are surrounded by situations and circumstances that exist to create increase in your life."

Discover Your Dream

- When your opportunity-detection skills are honed and you can spot opportunities, the *way* in which you respond becomes critical. Your approach is determined by what is happening inside you.

- Every opportunity is tied to your purpose, and every threat can also be a gift. When you are faced with an obstacle, potential setback, or fear about either, allow it to make you stronger, smarter, more alert, and better prepared for your destiny.

- Awareness is required to recognize and seize opportunities that can lead to the fulfillment of your strategic life plan.

Define Your Dream

An opportunity doesn't become a reality unless and until you make the conscious choice to embrace it and act upon it. But some opportunities fall under the category of distractions. Answer the following questions when discerning between opportunity and distraction:

Does the opportunity dovetail with the things you want to achieve? _____

Why do you want explore this opportunity?

_____

_____

_____

Does the opportunity cost seem reasonable in the pursuit of your dream?

_____

_____

_____

Can the opportunity be reasonably pursued and are key factors related to the opportunity within your control?

_____

_____

_____

Does the opportunity promote intimacy, engage your spirituality, and promote generativity?

_____

_____

_____

Declare Your Dream

Declare that you will take advantage of every opportunity placed in front of you. First you will discern it, then you will take action, then you will either learn from success or learn from failure. Learning is good either way.

Develop Your Dream

Are you living in survival mode—devoting your energy to crisis management rather than dream development? What steps can you take to become more proactive and prevent crises that zap your energy and stymie your dreams?

_____

_____

_____

Dedicate Your Dream

The best opportunities are those provided by God. Being close to Him allows you to discern more readily the doors He is holding open for you. Dedicate your path to Him today.

Remember: "Regardless of how your opportunity originates, it is your response that translates the growth potential it offers into realized increase. The important fact to remember is that all opportunities, even crises, are potential growth opportunities."

TRANSFORM POSSIBILITY INTO PROBABILITY

"The vision of your completed dream bridges another important span—the gulf between present and future—and in some ways erases the distinctions between the two. With your vision established, your thought-life places you at the end of the story so that, in a sense, your dream must catch up with you."

Discover Your Dream

- Your response to an opportunity has great bearing on the degree to which your strategic life plan is realized. Be sure to develop in your mind a clear picture of where you see the opportunity taking you—before you act.

- In order to effectively turn possibility (opportunity) into probability and to do so without compromising your overall mission and well-being, be willing to uncover any conflicts between your strategic life plan and any opportunity that arises.

- Be sure that your assessment of opportunities is reasoned and not overly emotional.

Define Your Dream

"More than any other action taken or choice made, belief is the element that will bring your dream to fruition." Consider the following statements and write your thoughts about each:

Belief applied to an idea or other opportunity produces possibility.

_____

_____

_____

Belief applied to possibility produces a plan which makes the possible probable.

_____

_____

_____

Belief applied to what is probable keeps the vision alive, so that probability becomes reality.

_____

_____

_____

When opportunity knocks, you have every right to seize it.

_____

_____

_____

Be decisive and strongly intentional. Don't procrastinate in the face of an opportunity.

_____

_____

_____

Declare Your Dream

Decisive people are intentional people. About possibilities turning into probabilities, ask: *Why here?* and *Why now?* You will maintain a strong sense of intentionality based on your mission.

Develop Your Dream

"Belief is the glue that holds your dreams and opportunities together—and it is the substance that bridges the gap between opportunity and probability." What kind of glue is holding your dreams and opportunities together?

_____

_____

_____

Dedicate Your Dream

And looking at them Jesus said to them, "With people this is impossible, but with God all things are possible" (Matthew 19:26).

Remember: "Supersizing the positive will help you get the most out of every opportunity. It will also keep your perspective and your spirits elevated, making the journey more enjoyable."

WEEK

4

STOP SOLVING PROBLEMS AND START CREATING SOLUTIONS

"The ability to generate a new reality is what distinguishes the creation of solutions from the mere solving of problems."

Discover Your Dream

- Problem solving falls short because it rivets our attention on the problem instead of the context in which it was formed.
- Solution creation is not a limiting function; instead it dissolves boundaries and increases opportunity.
- Truly creative solutions come from people willing to test a unique mindset. The solution then creates a new mindset for others.

Define Your Dream

Solution creation requires active participation, awareness, thoughtfulness, and a balanced approach to risk tolerance.

Do you consider yourself a solution creator who focuses on the possibilities rather than on the problems? Why or why not?

_____

_____

_____

Can you embrace the present moment to create what never existed before?

_____

_____

_____

Is it your habit to use problems (and other negative outcomes) to set yourself free from old limitations?

_____

_____

_____

Are you one who doesn't wait to be rescued by others; instead you see yourself as resourceful—able to think, act, and get results in every situation?

_____

_____

_____

Have you fired the paradigm "gatekeeper" stationed in the guardhouse between your ears—and in the minds of others?

_____

_____

_____

Declare Your Dream

Rather than looking for approval from others, solution creators—you—look within with an eye on life's purpose, dreams, and values. Be confident.

Develop Your Dream

"Because your strategic life plan is written with your authentic dream in mind, it is a document of solutions. Why? Because your dream is a solution to something...for somebody...somewhere." Do you believe your dream is a solution? What possibilities can you identify?

_____

_____

_____

Dedicate Your Dream

The same problem may have been plaguing you for years. Believing that you can create a solution is the first step to becoming victorious over that problem.

Remember: "You are a walking, breathing solution to something, and when it comes to handling life's problems, you fall into one of two categories: you are either a full-blown, problem-plundering solution creator ...or you are in the process of becoming one!"

LIVE YOUR DREAM-POWERED, STRATEGIC LIFE

"Your dream may already be carefully framed in your heart. If not, it is percolating just beneath your emotional skin, where it is ready to erupt in a flow of words and images that will forecast your future and guide your destiny path . . . until the clock stops running and the scoreboard reads Game Over."

Discover Your Dream

- The vision of your fulfilled destiny motivates you from within. Your desire to achieve your mission is the renewable resource refreshed by your purpose in life.

- Keep your attitudes, speech, and actions positive. This is easier when your source of motivation is pure and your want-to is amply supplied.

- Maintain a clear vision of your future in good times and in not-so-good times. Your dream is a powerfully motivating snapshot of your future—keep it in focus. Rehearse your mission statement daily; read your strategic life plan often.

- Recognize the milestones en route to your dream. Maintain a clear sense of where you came from, where you are, and where you are heading. Take ownership of your journey by being fully aware of your progress.

- Assign a high priority to vision-oriented activities. To achieve your dream, daily remind yourself of your priorities. Allow your goals to dictate the content of your consciousness so your priorities will be refreshed and aligned with your purpose. Don't allow distractions to sidetrack you.

Define Your Dream

"Your strategic life plan is your primary source. Your mission statement will guide your development of organizing principles designed to help you make smart choices."

Are you aware of and open to new career opportunities? Why or why not?

_____

_____

_____

Have you taken advantage of the personal and professional development opportunities that have come your way? Why or why not?

_____

_____

_____

Have you developed a daily work schedule that accommodates your strategic life plan? Why or why not?

_____

_____

_____

Have you identified areas in which you want to strengthen or grow your skills and talents? Why or why not?

_____

_____

_____

Have you realized the importance of effectively working with others and developing a sense of teamwork? Why or why not?

_____

_____

_____

Declare Your Dream

Living your dream along with a mentor can be very educational, challenging, motivating, and helpful. Think back to those you've shared your goals and dream with, and choose someone who will be an encourager.

Develop Your Dream

"Your desire ability to learn from a mentoring relationship rests largely in your attraction to what the mentor knows and is able to model for you. But this relationship must be reciprocal. Your mentor will be attracted by the opportunity to awaken the elements revealed in your destiny code. . . . " What are your fears about exposing your dreams and goals with a mentor? Are you willing to overcome those fears?

_____

_____

_____

Dedicate Your Dream

Your life-long Mentor who is ever-present and ever-loving has your best interests in mind always. When you dedicate your life and your destiny to Him, you will see amazing results—today, tomorrow, and until the day you take your last breath.

Remember: "Your destiny awaits; it will be fulfilled by you or not at all. It will be enjoyed by you or by no one. It will speak to the miracle of your creation and will fulfill your every desire. While there is still breath in your lungs *you, and only you, can live your dream.*"

Additional copies of this book and other
book titles from DESTINY IMAGE are
available at your local bookstore.

Call toll-free: 1-800-722-6774.

Send a request for a catalog to:

Destiny Image® Publishers, Inc.

P.O. Box 310
Shippensburg, PA 17257-0310

*"Speaking to the Purposes of God for This
Generation and for the Generations to Come."*

For a complete list of our titles,
visit us at www.destinyimage.com.